Preaching Through Joshua

A Series of 19 exegetical sermons from book of Joshua.

by Pastor Paul Wallace

Note to reader: This book is not intended to be a commentary, rather it is a collection of sermons through the book of Joshua excluding the distribution of the land to the tribes. I have focused on applications to our lives under the New Covenant initiated by out Lord Jesus Christ. It is meant to be an inspiration to those individuals who are interested in studying Joshua as well a tool for those who would teach and preach this inspired book of the Bible

Dedicated to my assistant pastor Luke Thorne. It has been a blessing to mentor him. He came on the staff at just the right time for him and for the church. His God given abilities have expanded the outreach of the church and been a special help during the COVID crisis. I hope I have been like a mentoring Moses to him and look forward to see him find his Joshua like calling. Joshua 1:8

Contents

A New Leader Joshua 1:1-3

God gave Israel the five books of the Law, the Torah, through His servant Moses. Those books focused on God calling out a people for Himself. They tell of the dramatic story of God raising up a deliverer: Moses. God used the insecure underdog who had once fled from Egypt to save his life to deliver His people from the greatest world power. Moses led the children of Israel through forty years in the wilderness while God miraculously provided food and water for the entire nation. He dealt with their constant complaining. He interceded for them when they rebelled against God. He brought them God's rules for their nation. But then within sight of the Promised Land, Moses, the servant of God died.

¹ After the death of Moses the servant of the LORD, the LORD said to Joshua the son of Nun, Moses' assistant, ² "Moses my servant is dead. Now therefore arise, go over this Jordan, you and all this people, into the land that I am giving to them, to the people of Israel. Joshua 1:1,2 The people of Israel often failed to listen to Moses on the way to the Promised Land. God had communicated with Moses a tiny portion of the bigger picture. There was coming another man from this nation who would be like Moses, only to this One they *must* listen (Deuteronomy 18:15). They referred to this One who was to come as The Prophet (John 1:21).

Their experiences with Moses were foreshadowing something much greater. A Deliverer from the bondage of sin was coming. He would lead them through the wilderness of life to the promised land of heaven. But in God's plan, that deliverance was to take place in the land to which they were going. The One to whom they must listen would not fail to lead them all the way in, unlike Moses who died in the wilderness. The coming One was given the same name as the man who led the people after Moses died, Joshua (*Yehoshua* meaning YHWH saves), or as Jews would later say the name in Aramaic, *Yeshua*. That is what the angel Gabriel told Mary to name her child (Luke 1:31). The Greek form is *Iesous* (Jesus - see Acts 7:45; Hebrews 4:8), which is also Greek for Joshua. We can see the hand of God orchestrating history to prepare people for Jesus' first coming. It is not that Jesus happens to have the same name as Joshua, but rather that Jesus orchestrated history to point us to what He would do.

We should see this book we are starting a journey through as a step in God's plan to save mankind, a metaphor for Jesus leading us to heaven. Abraham and his son and grandson were promised that they would become a great nation, that they would possess the land of Canaan, and bless the world (Genesis 22:17,18). Just as Joshua brought about the fulfillment of the physical promises to Abraham to possess the land, so the second Joshua brought to fruition the spiritual part of the prophecy to bless the world through Abraham's descendant (1 Corinthians 15:46; Genesis 22:18; Galatians 3:13,14). This second Joshua had to be born in the land of promise in a town called Bethlehem, the house of bread (Micah 5:2). He had to minister in Galilee according to the words of the prophet Isaiah (Isaiah 9:1,2). He would redeem not only Israel, but all who will come to Him in faith (Isaiah 49:6; Matthew 1:21). He would suffer and die, but He would conquer our greatest enemy in the process (Genesis 3:15). In our conclusion to Luke, we saw how Jesus defeated death!

The land of Canaan into which Joshua was leading them was filled with vile practices, people who had rejected the words of Melchizedek, the King of Righteousness and Peace (Hebrews 7:1-4), a people who had to be judged first so that the Jews could occupy it without being corrupted by their lurid worship practices (Deuteronomy 12:31). The Book of Joshua tells us how this occupation came about.

The book has three main sections: the conquest of Canaan in chapters one through twelve, and the division of the land as God promised in chapters thirteen to twenty-two. We will skim over that section as it is a list of detailed boundaries of each tribe. The conclusion is in chapters twenty-three and twenty-four. In those chapters Israel is exhorted to remain faithful to the Lord so that they might enjoy God's blessings. We will be focusing on fourteen of the twenty-four chapters.

Joshua had led the army of Israel against their foes in the wilderness. He was Moses right hand man. He was the one waiting for Moses when he came down from Mount Sinai with the commandments. Joshua had forty years to observe and learn from Moses. Now the time had come for him to lead. The training was over.

I imagine that Joshua was excited, for the nation stood at the edge of what had been promised to them when Abraham had left Ur centuries before (1406 B.C. 1 Kings 6:1). But would God speak to Joshua as He had with Moses? Joshua knew their victories and survival were all due to the God who led them, the God of Abraham, Isaac, and Jacob. He is a covenant keeping God, and He had covenanted to give the land to Abraham's descendants (Genesis 15:18-20).

Joshua had been in the land once before. He told of how fertile it was. He was ready to go in then, but the other spies told of the giant people whose size made the Hebrews appear as grasshoppers. The people were afraid and refused to go in, though Joshua and Caleb had insisted God would give them victory (Numbers 14:8). Now the second opportunity to receive the promise had come.

Joshua knew this day was coming. In Deuteronomy 31, Moses told the people *³ The LORD your God himself will go over before you. He will destroy these nations before you, so that you shall dispossess them, and Joshua will go over at your head, as the LORD has spoken.* To know that the LORD would go before them was all the assurance Joshua needed. But Joshua also knew the many times the people of Israel had rebelled against God's will. The older generation had died out and the new generation had seen God's judgments fall on their fathers. They had learned from their failures and were more eager to follow the Lord. It had taken them forty years in the wilderness to purge out most of the rebellion and bring them to the place where they were ready to receive the promise.

Both command and promise depend upon the sovereignty of God, expressed in his wise will and achieved by his irresistible power. So it is as God's people both believe the promises and obey the commands that they enter into the experience of fellowship with God at the deepest, relational level. The same is true for us today. Why do we so often fail to obey God's commands? Because we do not really believe his promises. The two always go together. Faith leads to obedience. Disobedience is always rooted in distrust. We will see this lesson worked out often in the book of Joshua; it is a continuing challenge that we shall often encounter in our contemporary experience of living the Christian life.[i]

I want to digress for a moment to point out the typology in those words of Moses. Remember that Joshua is the Hebrew name for Jesus. Crossing the Jordan River is symbolic of death. It was the end of one way of life and the beginning of the new. Manna would stop. They went from the promise to the fulfillment. The LORD would go over before them. Jesus our Lord did pass through death before us. He is the head of the church. He leads us into the promised land, life in Christ. He will drive out our enemies: the world, the flesh, and the devil. What a picture in that one declaration, "God Himself will go over before you!"

We can see the same parallel in Moses' prayer for a successor. *16 "Let the LORD, the God of the spirits of all flesh, appoint a man over the congregation. 17 who shall go out before them and come in before them, who shall lead them out and bring them in, that the congregation of the LORD may not be as sheep that have no shepherd." 18 So the LORD said to Moses, "Take Joshua the son of Nun, a man in whom is the Spirit, and lay your hand on him.* Numbers 27:16-18 Moses had Joshua at his side for forty years, and yet he asked God to appoint the right man to take his place. He asked for someone with a shepherd's heart to guide them. God affirmed that it was Joshua because the Spirit of God was in him. But the ultimate answer to Moses' prayer is our great Shepherd, Jesus (John 10:11). He leads us out and brings us in. He has the Spirit without measure in Him.

Joshua was described as Moses' assistant in Exodus 24:13. He went up Mount Sinai with Moses as far as he was allowed. He was with Moses when he came down the mountain with the tablets. When Moses would go the tent of meeting - a type of the future tabernacle, it was Joshua who would stay behind at the tent even after Moses had left speaking with God (Exodus 33:11). It is important that God's leaders not only desire to hear from God, but that they love to be in His presence.

Verse one calls Moses "the servant of the LORD" and the book of Joshua will conclude by naming Joshua as "the servant of the LORD" (Joshua 24:29). That tells us that this book is just as inspired as the Torah. Why would the promise in the Torah be any more important than the fulfillment in Joshua? The book of Joshua is the complement to the Torah. It tells us that God is faithful to His Word. We can trust that God *always* brings His promises to pass. In fact, some people claim the Torah should include Joshua.

If there was any concern about leading the people into the Promised Land, it was the giants they had seen when they first spied out the land (Numbers 13:33). But Joshua had seen that the battle belongs to the Lord. We first meet Joshua when the Amalekites attacked Israel in the wilderness. Joshua led the battle. But the battle was won by Moses' hands uplifted to God. Joshua's first great victory and reputation came because of intercession. He quickly learned that the source of power is God (Exodus 17:11). When Joshua led the Israelites to victory over Bashan and the Amorites Moses told Joshua that God would do the same with all the nations in the Promised Land. He was told not to fear them, for God would fight for him (Deuteronomy 3:21,22).

Deuteronomy ends with Moses assuring Joshua and the nation that God would give them victory with Joshua leading them. The most important theme is that God is with them and goes before them. That is why Joshua can be strong and courageous. That is why he did not need to fear the giants. Moses told Joshua the promise that he had once received, that God would never leave or forsake him (Deuteronomy 31:8).

Brothers and sisters, the promise is ours in Jesus. In fact, the author of Hebrews tells us the same promise is ours (Hebrews 13:5; John 10:28,29). That is why we should be strong and courageous and never fear what we must face. Our God is the same God who was with Joshua. He has already gone before us and given us the victory over our greatest enemies, Satan and death. The skirmishes in this life may seem difficult, but the main battle is already won, and heaven is ours in Christ Jesus who is always with us. That is why we can be joyful even facing minor defeats. The Lamb always wins in the end. There is no power that compares!

The book of Joshua will often point to the fact that it is the Lord who gives us the victory. It is pointing to faith in God and His Word, not the man Joshua. It would be easy to imagine Joshua as a giant muscle-bound man with superhuman skills and the courage of a lion. If that was the case, why do the Scriptures command him to be strong and courageous five different times (Deuteronomy 31:6,7,23; Joshua 1:6,9)? It reminds me of Saul and David. Saul was head and shoulders taller than his brothers, but David was short in stature. Saul was eventually rejected by God and we remember little David as the great warrior king of Israel. But it was because God was with him, for David was a man after God's own heart (1 Samuel 13:14).

Paul reminds us in 2 Corinthians 4:7 that *we have this treasure in jars of clay, to show that the surpassing power belongs to God and not to us*. One of the faults of the church in our age is the dependence on man, on human initiative, and on clever ideas. For many people, church is a commercial enterprise. The battle is for more attendees rather than against the darkness of this world. God honors faithfulness, not numbers.

Joshua's leadership was different from that of Moses in that he had the Word of God to guide him and the established priesthood to hear from God. Today we have the written Word and all who are in Christ have become His priests (1 Peter 2:5). All who are in Christ have the indwelling Holy Spirit to be our wisdom and guide. We still have elders as the nation of Israel had, but they are dependent on the written Word of God and the Spirit within them. Instead of one man as the head, we have Christ Jesus as the head and the elders as under-shepherds (1 Timothy 5:17). This is how we confront the darkness in the world today. We make disciples as Jesus instructed us (Matthew 28:19). One soul at a time is brought into the kingdom and then built up with the Word and fellowship. It is the work of God in their hearts. He does use us as instruments, but just like the book of Joshua declares, the battle is the Lord's. It is by faith and trust that we obey the leading of the Spirit and march forward to claim the land.

As victorious and faithful as Joshua was, he was only a foreshadow of One greater to come, for after his death, the people began to turn to idolatry. We need a place of rest that will endure forever and where God is worshiped forever. A place of rest was promised to Israel, and yet it did not come to pass under the first Joshua. The author of Hebrews writes, *For if Joshua had given them rest, God would not have spoken of another day later on. So then, there remains a Sabbath rest for the people of God, for whoever has entered God's rest has also rested from his works as God did from his. Let us therefore strive to enter that rest, so that no one may fall by the same sort of disobedience.* (Hebrews 4:8-11) The second Joshua, Jesus, tells us *28 Come to me, all who labor and are heavy laden, and I will give you rest.* Matthew 11:28 Throughout the book of Joshua we will see these patterns played out in our daily lives.

We should consider that a number of great men of God have recently passed on. Billy Graham, Bill Bright, and Ravi Zacharias have gone to their reward. And though God may raise up others to take their places, we already have the greatest leader, for we already have the second Joshua, Jesus! And He is all we need! He is the head of the church. He is leading us into the promised land and has already gone before us into battle and defeated the giants.

In our study in the Gospel of John, we learned that the disciples were not spiritual elites. They were common people. You will enjoy watching The Chosen as it really emphasizes their humanity. A rabbi of that day never would have chosen them. But Jesus did. As youth, they failed to go on and learn all a good Jewish boy hoping to become a rabbi would learn. They thought they were only fit for common labor. One was even a despised IRS agent! What is Jesus doing selecting men like that? He spent the night in prayer before He chose them (Luke 6:12,13). He did what the Father directed Him to do. But why these common men? Because they realized they didn't deserve to be chosen. Do you realize that? But God chose you and me anyway (Deuteronomy 7:7,8). It is because it brings greater glory to God! It is because we are more dependent on His life in us rather than our own intellect and ability (Zechariah 4:6).

Listen to how the Apostle Paul explained it. *26 For consider your calling, brothers: not many of you were wise according to worldly standards, not many were powerful, not many were of noble birth. 27 But God chose what is foolish in the world to shame the wise; God chose what is weak in the world to shame the strong; 28 God chose what is low and despised in the world, even things that are not, to bring to nothing things that are, 29 so that no human being might boast in the presence of God. 30 And because of him you are in Christ Jesus, who became to us wisdom from God, righteousness and sanctification and redemption, 31 so that, as it is written, "Let the one who boasts, boast in the Lord."* 1 Corinthians 1:26-31

What can you do of eternal significance on your own? ZERO! We need Jesus' life in us and through us, anointing us for the good works He has planned in advance for us to do (Ephesians 2:10). Victorious living is relying on Jesus, moment by moment! Most of our life is the process of learning to do just that. Great leaders have died, our beloved mentors have passed on, and now it is time for

Joshua/Jesus to take over in our lives and touch the world with His love through us.

Questions:
1 What is the background to this book?
2 What is this true story foreshadowing?
3 Who did Moses tell the people to watch for?
4 What are the three sections of the book?
5 What had Joshua learned under Moses?
6 How does belief and obedience affect our relationship with God?
7 What was Moses' prayer for the next leader? Who was it?
8 What is the most important theme in the book?
9 How are we led today?
10 Why does God work through seemingly insignificant people?

Be Strong and Courageous Joshua 1:4-9

Last week we looked at the transition in leadership from Moses to Joshua. We saw how Joshua was the same as the name for Jesus who leads us into the ultimate promised land. We also considered the fact that these transitions take place in our lives as well. Those who mentor us and have been godly examples to us in time graduate to their place in the heavenly realm, and we are left to pick up the torch and stand in the gap they leave. The instructions to Joshua resonate with us, reminding us what we must do if we are to be successful to fulfill the destiny God has for us.

In our passage for today, God is speaking instruction and encouragement to Joshua. He had just promised that every place the soles of his feet trod would be conquered. God continued by describing the extent of the land He was giving them. *⁴ From the wilderness and this Lebanon as far as the great river, the river Euphrates, all the land of the Hittites to the Great Sea toward the going down of the sun shall be your territory.* Joshua 1:4 God described the area that was to belong to Israel as He had described it to Abraham in Genesis 15:18-20. Even under kings David and Solomon, it would cover only a part of what is described here. The northern boundary is Lebanon, the eastern is the Euphrates, the western is the Mediterranean. Numbers 34:3 tells us the southern boundary is the southern tip of the Dead Sea. The national boundaries today go further south to the Red Sea, but the eastern boundary is a tiny fraction of what is described here. David Oginde tells us, *"In terms of current political boundaries, the promised land would thus cover modern Israel, the whole of Jordan, a large part of Saudi Arabia, half of Iraq, the whole of Lebanon, part of Syria and the whole of Kuwait."*[ii]

What happened? Every place Joshua's soles trod was given to them, but they got comfortable and settled down. Even within the boundaries of what is today called Israel, the Canaanites remained. They became a thorn in Israel's side, and their idols lured Israel away from faith in God. It was their lack of faith in God that kept them from receiving all God had promised them (Hebrews 3:19). What a warning for us today to never stop taking the spiritual land in our own hearts and in our families and culture!

Comfort and compromise often tempt us to stop short of partaking in all of God's generous promises. Think of the difference in the world today if they had taken all that land. Most of their enemies would not exist. There would be no struggle for space. They would have huge oil reserves. Instead, those things made their enemies wealthy.

In the spiritual realm the same is true for us. If we don't take the spiritual land, press the fight onward, we settle for far less than God has for us. Families face crises on their own because they refuse to become part of a family of God. We cave in to temptations because we have not become strong in God's Word. Nor do we have the joy of seeing souls won because our hearts are set on the passing things of this world that never satisfy. And so, we become discouraged with this life and disappointed in the things the world offers and miss the encouragement, peace, and joy of life in Christ.

Pastor David Jackman tells us that *Because there is never any shortage of power or depletion of God's purpose on his part, it must be true that none of us has less of God and his promised blessings than we truly desire.*[iii] As I have said before, "Our wanter is broken." Our desires are so wrapped up in the temporal that we miss the spiritual blessings of God that include peace in our souls. We will not do what Jesus instructs us to do. *Come to me all you who are weary and burdened and I will give you rest* (Matthew 11:28). Instead, we go to our own efforts and go about our own way that only makes matters worse. Our purpose is to glorify God and enjoy Him forever. Because He has put His very nature in us, we are expected to do just that! Beware of forgetting the purpose for your existence (2 Peter 3:17). May God give us a passion and hunger for more of God and to experience the promises of God.

The people of Canaan had superior weaponry. There were still giants in the land. Some of them had walled cities. They had alliances to help one another against Israel. That had to be daunting. But Joshua had the promises of God, and so do we. We look at our entertainment industry and educational system of indoctrination and our task seems impossible. But never forget the promises of God. If we remain in Christ, we will bear much fruit (John 15:5). God is always superior in power to anything the world can throw at us. Let us not be found to fall short of taking all the spiritual territory the Lord has for us. Because others do not do so does not excuse our disobedience.

⁵ No man shall be able to stand before you all the days of your life. Just as I was with Moses, so I will be with you. I will not leave you or forsake you. Joshua 1:5 These three sentences are three powerful promises Joshua must have held dear to His heart. The first was that no man would be able to stand before him. That means that every enemy soldier he encountered would fall. Battles then were hand to hand. Imagine how hearts pounded when lines of warriors clashed. One wrong move and you are dead. In every encounter it was to the death. Joshua is getting old. He has had a lot of battle experience, and God is telling him he will continue to be successful in every encounter. How that must have encouraged him to be confident in battle.

What battles are you facing right now? During this epidemic there are many. Whatever it is, never forget that Jesus is with you. That is the next statement. *Just as I was with Moses, so I will be with you.* Moses counted on God's presence and would not move without it (Exodus 33:14-16). This does not mean God would speak to Joshua face to face like He did with Moses. We see a very different relationship. He will meet with Joshua in the form of the Angel of the LORD. He will speak to Joshua through the Scriptures and the High Priest. Each of us has our own way of communing with the Lord, but the Word of God is the plumbline for us all (Isaiah 8:20). It is the revelation of God's promises and purposes.

You say, but pastor, Moses was special. What made Moses special? It was his communion with God. From the burning bush to the tent of meeting, Moses heard from God and obeyed. Well, Jesus said, *"My sheep hear my voice, and they follow me"* (John 10:4). Isn't that the same thing? Our problem is that we often refuse to take the time to be still, to read the Scriptures and wait on God to speak to us. If we want to see the fruit of the promise, the victorious presence of Christ in us, we need to take the time to listen and then obey.

And the third promise is that God would never leave or forsake him. We are assured in the New Testament that those who are in Christ have the same promise. He is with us. It is no less real than how God was with Moses or how we will read of how He was with Joshua. He has promised to never leave us or forsake us just as He promised Joshua (Hebrews 13:5). That should give us great courage as it gave Joshua. Joshua knew that if God is for us, who can be against us (Romans 8:31)? We need not fear anything that God allows in our lives. He is with us and will never forsake us, for we have been adopted into the family of God (Matthew 29:20; Romans 8:15). That should be the comfort and confidence we live in moment by moment. The all-powerful God of the universe loves us and is with us. He will see you through whatever He allows in your life (1 Corinthians 10:13).

6 Be strong and courageous, for you shall cause this people to inherit the land that I swore to their fathers to give them. Joshua 1:6 Joshua is to be strong and courageous for he shall (that is with that courage and strength he will) cause God's people to inherit the land in fulfillment of the 400-year-old promise to Abraham, a promise repeated to Isaac and Jacob. It is important that we understand that a part of the promise is not only the land, but also a blessing that would come out of that land to bless the world (Genesis 12:3). And of course, that blessing is Jesus.

When Joseph's father Jacob, whose name was changed to Israel, was dying, he asked that his bones be buried in the Promised Land (Genesis 50:5). When Joseph was dying, he made his brothers promise that when God came to their aid to then take his bones and bury them in the Promised Land. Archeologists found the small pyramid in which they believe his bones were kept until they were carried to the Promised Land as Joseph had requested. At that location in Goshen, they found remains of a statue that had worn a coat of many colors. The Israelites had lived with this promise of the land for 400 years and now Joshua is about to finally lead them to the fulfillment.

And you thought some promises in your life were taking a long time to come to pass! We who live in the microwave age with instant communication around the world are too easily upset when something takes longer than expected. God knows the right time. If it is a request according to His will, and if it does not violate the will of the person you are praying for, it will happen in God's perfect time. God told Abraham it would be generations later as the iniquity of the Amorites had to come to the level of impending judgment. Then their conquest of the land would be righteous judgment.

I have seen prayers answered in minutes and others that were only answered after years of waiting. And sometimes God does not answer in ways that we can observe. This 400-year-old promise we are reading about should remind us that God is never in a hurry.

7 Only be strong and very courageous, being careful to do according to all the law that Moses my servant commanded you. Do not turn from it to the right hand or to the left, that you may have good success wherever you go. Joshua 1:7 His courage and strength were to be focused on living according to the revelation God gave to Moses, the first five books of our Bible. There is a series of instructions directing this focus. The first is to carefully do *all* of the commands in the Word. He can't use it in a cafeteria fashion, picking which parts he will obey and which he will ignore. Total obedience is required of him if he wishes to succeed.

While we are no longer under the 613 laws of the old covenant (Romans 8:2-4), Jesus does give us quite a few commands in the Gospels. Unlike the old laws that dictated what you could eat and wear, society rules, and worship instructions in order to be an example as a godly nation that would be blessed with prosperity, the commands of Jesus are descriptions of what our new life in Him should be like. The promise is not physical prosperity but communion with God, a restoration of what was lost in the Garden when Adam and Eve walked with God (Genesis 3:8). When we obey, we have fellowship with Jesus! That is better than any physical prosperity promised under the Old Covenant. It is the blessing of the fruits of the Spirit, peace in the storms of life, assurance in spiritual battles, and joy inexpressible and full of glory (1 Peter 1:8)!

But when we disobey that communion is broken. God withdraws from communing with us when we are in rebellion. It is a sign to us that something is wrong. Our peace fades (Colossians 3:15). Worry sets in. We become anxious and try to figure out what we can do, instead of going to prayer and getting God's answer. And in many cases, it is because we have an idea what God would tell us, and we don't want to hear it.

One example is forgiveness. We have determined we will not forgive someone when God has told us we must, for we have been forgiven (Matthew 6:14,15). Another is our complaint over hardships. Jesus told us to take up our cross and follow Him (Matthew 16:24). But we often decide we want more comfortable lives, and we refuse to go where He is leading or give what He is asking of us. The Apostle Paul tells us to pray without ceasing (1 Thessalonians 5:17), but we want to relegate it to ten minutes in the morning and before we eat. Brothers and sisters if we want to be victorious in this battle of taking the land for the kingdom of God in the hearts of men and women, we need to obey the Commander. Or in the words of this verse, be careful to observe all that God has commanded us. That is when we will have success wherever we go!

8 This Book of the Law shall not depart from your mouth, but you shall meditate on it day and night, so that you may be careful to do according to all that is written in it. For then you will make your way prosperous, and then you will have good success. Joshua 1:8 Then Joshua is told that he is not to turn one way or the other from that written Word. No compromise is allowed if he wants good success. There is no room for his own ideas that contradict a command. Success is dependent on complete obedience.

Following that is the command in verse 8 to talk about God's Word all the time and meditate in it day and night. This reminds us of God's commands in the Shema - to put the Law as frontlets on our foreheads and bind them to our arms, to speak of them when we go out and when we come in, and to teach them to our children (Deuteronomy 6:4-9). And the purpose stated here was so that they would then be careful to do it all. Then they would find that they would prosper and be successful. Their prosperity and success were to show the surrounding nations that the God of Israel was the only true God. It was to prompt in the nations a desire to learn about Him.

If that command to meditate in the Word day and night was true for Joshua when only the initial revelation of God was in writing, to what extent should we value the entire revelation we have received in the Bible? Wycliffe sent out a plea for funds to follow up in areas where only a portion of the Word was translated. They had translated the Gospel of John, but for decades that was all that linguistic group had and they were begging for more. We have numerous English translations of the entire Bible and they sit on shelves gathering dust. We have Bibles everywhere, in hotels, hospitals, homes, and yet they go unread and unappreciated. The Word is so rarely brought up in conversation for fear someone might be offended. When was the last time you heard someone say, "Jesus said in the Gospel of Mark that we are to…" I was so blessed when one of the young adults asked me, "What is God showing you today?" I hadn't had anyone ask me that in years. When was the last time you asked that of a brother or sister in Christ? Are we taking time to let God show us things in His Word?

There is a famine for hearing the Word of the Lord just as was predicted by the prophet Amos (Amos 8:11), but it is not because it is not available. It is because we are too preoccupied with the things of daily life. We don't take this command personally and set aside the time to hear from God.

Is this promise for us as well? If we as the body of Christ will speak of it always and meditate in it day and night, would we not see our faith prosper and have success against our culture's decline? We pray for revival and repentance, but then do we change our ways? What we need to make this happen is the same thing Joshua needed, to be strong and courageous to do it! There is no time to start like today.

⁹ Have I not commanded you? Be strong and courageous. Do not be frightened, and do not be dismayed, for the LORD your God is with you wherever you go." Joshua 1:9 Allow me to rephrase that verse. Has not God command us to be strong and bold? Do not be frightened of people or dismayed at their reactions, for Jesus our Savior and the Holy Spirit who are one is our God and will be with us wherever we go! And if God is with us then who can be against us (Romans 8:31)! Do we believe it? Belief is demonstrated by action. I can say I believe it, but if I do not act accordingly, it is just wishful thinking, an untried concept of which I am uncertain (James 1:6,7).

Like Joshua, we face what seems to be impossible odds. We can stay in the desert and live a meager spiritual life, or we can believe God and march into the spiritual promised land of life in Christ, believing God is with us and will give us victory. But that is only if we talk about the Word and meditate on it continually. Yes, we have the Holy Spirit to direct us, but the saints have discovered that His main directions come from the illumination of God's Word as we read and meditate on it. He brings the Scriptures to our minds in the situations we face. But if the Word is not hidden in our hearts, if our speech is always about politics or finances or temporal things, and we never take time to read and contemplate the application of God's Word, there is nothing in our memory from which the Spirit can draw to speak to us. Jesus told us that the Spirit reminds us of what He has already said (John 14:26). The Holy Spirit can teach us without the Word, but how will we know we are listening to the right voice if we do not take what we think we are hearing and check it with the Scriptures?

There are Christians who want the Holy Spirit to guide their every move, but they do not study the Word to know whether it is the Spirit speaking or their own inclinations. When they obey only to find chaos, they chalk it up to the Spirit doing something they do not understand. Well, that could be the case. But when it happens over and over, you would hope they would learn that it is not the Spirit they are listening to but their own inclinations. Zeal without a correct understanding of God's Word had the Apostle Paul killing Christians (Romans 10:2). He needed the Spirit to interpret the Word.

Do you want to be prosperous and successful for the kingdom of God? Then you need to read, meditate, and speak the Word of God. The difference between us and Joshua is that we have the revelation of Jesus in the New Testament and the indwelling Holy Spirit is always with us because of what Jesus has done for us. But notice that the LORD said He would be with Joshua wherever he went, and He still needed to devote himself to the Word of God.

How much of God's spiritual blessings do you desire? Will you fulfill the destiny God has for you? Let us be strong and courageous and go for it all! This dark world is in desperate need of shining lights to let them know there is hope in Jesus, eternal life in Jesus, and more love than they can imagine in our Lord and Savior Jesus, the Christ!

Questions:

1 What would be different if they believed God's promise and acted on it?

2 What would be different in our lives if we believed and acted on God's promises?

3 Do you believe the quote from Pastor Jackman?

4 What made Moses special?

5 Which promises in verse 5 are for us today?

6 Why does it take a long time for some prayers to be answered?

7 Why should we obey Jesus' commands?

8 Why do we avoid listening in prayer?

9 Does verse 8 apply to us? How?

10 How do we discern the voice of God?

Prepare for New Life Joshua 1:10-18

The Israelites were on the border of the Promised Land. Some of the tribes were going to remain in the land on the east side of the Jordan River but had promised to help their brothers take the land to the west. They had spied out the land before and knew it was fertile, but also knew that there were walled cities and giants that had to be overcome. The first time they came to this spot, fear overcame them, and they turned back. This time, the older generation has died out and the younger generation is ready to follow Moses' successor, Joshua, into the land. We saw how Joshua and Jesus have the same name, and the parallel of Joshua bringing the chosen people into the Promised Land just as our Joshua, Jesus, brings us into the kingdom of God.

In the previous verses God had spoken to Joshua and affirmed that he would be successful if he obeyed all the commands of Moses and would remain strong and courageous. This promise of a life that is blessed because of meditating on God's words is the theme of the first psalm. *[1] Blessed is the man who walks not in the counsel of the wicked, nor stands in the way of sinners, nor sits in the seat of scoffers; [2] but his delight is in the law of the LORD, and on his law he meditates day and night.* The word translated as law in this verse also means instructions. Psalm 1:1,2 tells us the blessings promised to Joshua are ours as well if we will meditate on God's instructions to us. The psalmist may have taken the concept from verse 8 in this chapter where Joshua was told to meditate day and night in the Law. We will find in our study of Joshua that his obedience to this instruction was the reason for his success.

The book of Joshua often points back to the words of Moses. In the same way, we will find our lives blessed if we meditate on the words of Scripture day and night. Jesus said we should live by every word that proceeds from the mouth of God (Matthew 4:4). In the Great Commission Jesus told us to make disciples of all nations (Matthew 28:19,20). Then He described what that meant in the following verse which says, "teaching them to obey all that I have commanded you." So just as Joshua was to obey all Moses' commands which came from God, we too will find spiritual success if we obey all the commands from God given through His son Jesus.

10 And Joshua commanded the officers of the people, 11 "Pass through the midst of the camp and command the people, 'Prepare your provisions, for within three days you are to pass over this Jordan to go in to take possession of the land that the LORD your God is giving you to possess.'" Joshua 1:10,11 The Jordan was at flood stage. Recently we visited the new baptismal site near the Allenby Crossing in Israel. This was most likely the place where Jesus was baptized by John the Baptist (Matthew 3:14-16). It is the approximate area in which the Israelites crossed the Jordan. Stairs lead down to the river where groups performed baptisms. Near the top of the stairs, about twenty feet above the river was a wooden sign that showed how high the water had reached at the highest flood stage since the site was built. That is a lot of water!

God said to "arise, and go over this Jordan, you and all this people..." (Verse 2). He said He would be with him like He was with Moses (verse 5). And what did God do for them when Moses led them to the Red Sea? Yep, He parted the waters (Exodus 14:21). Without fear of the conditions and in obedience to God's command, Joshua told the officers to get the people ready to go. He gave them three days to pack up and get ready to leave the wilderness behind. God said Joshua would cause the people to inherit the land (verse 6), so Joshua acted on what God said despite the raging Jordan, walled cities, and giants. He had faith in God's word! He took God's instruction to heart: "Be strong and very courageous!"

I will remind you all the way through the book of Joshua that Joshua is a foreshadow of Jesus. Jesus was strong and very courageous and meditated day and night in the Scriptures. He only did what the Father showed Him (John 5:19). And when the situations in Jesus' life looked daunting if not impossible, He obeyed the Father: rebuking the religious leaders (Matthew 23:13-15), declaring the truth of Scripture, predicting His death and resurrection (Mark 8:31), and marching into Jerusalem the last time knowing it would lead to the cross (Mark 10:32,33). That was being strong and courageous against the flood of anger raging against Him. He is our example.

What is the opposite of courageous? It is to be fearful and discouraged. During this time of COVID and political turmoil we need to be strong and courageous because the One who was our example wants His strength and courage to be displayed in our lives! We are not islands. We all affect one another. Your fear and discouragement can cause others to become more fearful and discouraged. Jesus' peace and courage in you can cause others to be more peaceful and courageous. Circumstances have nothing to do with it. The Jordan was roaring, but faith looks at God, not circumstances.

I have stood at the side of Oak Creek when it was flooding like that and the very ground shakes as boulders the size of cars bounce down the creek bed. Joshua could have looked at the Jordan and said, "Sure thing Lord, as soon as the Jordan subsides, I will get right to it." But that is not what he did. He expressed a courageous faith in God. And that is what we need to do in our present circumstances. Don't look at the conditions! Look to the greatness of our God. Faith sees that God is bigger than whatever we face. Remember, He allowed you to be in your circumstances. You may not like them, and they may be the consequences of your sin, but that doesn't change the grace and power of God. He will use it for your good and His glory if you let Him, if you are strong and courageous enough to trust Him (Romans 8:28). Or perhaps I should say if you trust Him enough to be strong and courageous.

They were to get ready to leave behind the cloud leading them by day and the fire by night, the provision of manna every day, and the water from the rock. They were leaving one way of life and getting ready to enter another. It is very similar to what happens to us when we decide to follow Jesus. We don't realize God has led us step by step to the point of making that decision, but once we make the decision we enter into a whole new land. We find out there is a battle to be fought, spiritual land to be taken, and entering that land of rest God is giving us requires our obedient efforts. Following Jesus is not a bed of roses. It is a war. But is it also an adventure and life more abundant (John 10:10).

12 And to the Reubenites, the Gadites, and the half-tribe of Manasseh Joshua said, 13 "Remember the word that Moses the servant of the LORD commanded you, saying, 'The LORD your God is providing you a place of rest and will give you this land.' 14 Your wives, your little ones, and your livestock shall remain in the land that Moses gave you beyond the Jordan, but all the men of valor among you shall pass over armed before your brothers and shall help them, Joshua 1:12-14 The tribes of Reuben, Gad, and half the tribe of Manasseh wanted the grazing land on that side of the Jordan. Moses said they could possess it if the fighting men agreed to go into the Promised Land and help the other tribes conquer the region (Numbers 32). Joshua had witnessed the agreement and so now he was reminding them of it. He was being faithful to the words of Moses just as God commanded him. The women, children, and animals were all to stay behind. That means the men of those tribes would have to trust that God would protect them and their possessions during the years of conquest.

Estimates for the conquest of the land are around five to seven years. Can you imagine leaving your wife and children for seven years of battle? I can't! Some of the men in our armed forces have done that with multiple deployments. The men in those tribes knew this was the fulfillment of God's promise to the nation. They knew it was for their children and grandchildren and generations to come. People in that age thought more about their posterity than their immediate prosperity. Today most people seem to only care about the immediate future.

I often wonder why God called me out. I was just as sinful as the next guy, even more so because I knew better. Many of the people who went through the experiences I went through never fully recovered. I began to consider my ancestors. Some of them left a profound spiritual legacy. I didn't know it when I was born-again or even when God called me to ministry. It was only later that I read about them, and I could see the promises of God to those who are faithful affect the generations that follow (Exodus 20:6).

The men of those tribes were willing to give up years with their families and risk their lives in numerous battles to secure their families' physical future prosperity. How much more should we be strong and courageous to secure the spiritual future of our posterity? Do you pray for your children and grandchildren to know Christ and put Him first in their lives? Are you an example that they can follow? It is never too late to start! Even if you were not a good example in the past, a change in your life now can have a big impact.

¹⁵ *until the LORD gives rest to your brothers as he has to you, and they also take possession of the land that the LORD your God is giving them. Then you shall return to the land of your possession and shall possess it, the land that Moses the servant of the LORD gave you beyond the Jordan toward the sunrise."* Joshua 1:15 Those tribes were provided a place of rest with the help of their brothers and so they were to help the other tribes find their own place of rest. Then they could return to their homes and families in the east. Just because we have found peace and our place in God's calling for us does not mean we settle in and forget about our brothers and sisters. Just as others helped you find your calling, you and I need to help others find their place of rest in what Jesus has done for them and God's will for their lives.

The author of Hebrews picks up on this wording and notes that later in Psalms 95:7-11 the Israelites did not enter the rest God promised, but if they would hear God's voice and not harden their hearts, they could even now enter His rest. Just because God provides a place of rest for us in Jesus, we still need to hear His voice and not harden our hearts. *⁷ again he appoints a certain day, "Today," saying through David so long afterward, in the words already quoted, "Today, if you hear his voice, do not harden your hearts." ⁸ For if Joshua had given them rest, God would not have spoken of another day later on. ⁹ So then, there remains a Sabbath rest for the people of God, ¹⁰ for whoever has entered God's rest has also rested from his works as God did from his. ¹¹ Let us therefore strive to enter that rest, so that no one may fall by the same sort of disobedience.* Hebrews 4:7-11 If we hear God's voice in Jesus' teaching and do not harden our hearts, we can enter the rest of God.

The Hebrew thought was that God is still in the seventh day of creation and resting from His works. We are invited to enter that rest because Jesus did the work for us. It does not mean that we stop making any effort (2 Peter 1:5,6), but that the spiritual striving to please God is no longer our struggle. Jesus did it! It is finished! He took our sins and gave us His righteousness (2 Corinthians 5:21). We rest in what He accomplished. And even the work that we do, we do in His strength (Ephesians 6:10). Yes, we strive but our striving is to yield to His life and power in us. It is to keep our old life out of the way and let the new life in us be expressed in His power. That is striving to enter His rest. It is not a one-time thing. It is a continual yielding to Jesus' light and life in us. *To turn head faith into a personal possession is a fight always, not sometimes.*[iv]

[16] And they answered Joshua, "All that you have commanded us we will do, and wherever you send us we will go. [17] Just as we obeyed Moses in all things, so we will obey you. Only may the LORD your God be with you, as he was with Moses! Joshua 1:16,17 In that age, both Egyptians and the tribes of Palestine would pledge an oath to a new king who took the throne. While Israel's king was God, Joshua was His representative. They made a promise to follow Joshua's commands and go where he sends them. We must make the same promise to our Joshua, for once we tried to be our own king and found we were actually serving the evil one. When we accept Christ as King of kings, we make a similar pledge to serve Him rather than our fallen nature.

The Israelites added a strange caveat to their pledge. Just as they obeyed Moses, they would obey Joshua, *as long as* the Lord was with him as He was with Moses. Now, if we look back, their parents did not always obey. They must have been speaking for themselves personally. And so, we too can say that our ancestors have not always followed and obeyed, but neither have we. However, we can commit to do so now, realizing our weaknesses, but also realizing the help of the Holy Spirit and the power of the cross (1 John 1:9). Our Joshua always has God with Him for they are one (John 10:30).

Can you say those words to our Joshua this morning, "All that you have commanded us we will do and wherever you send us we will go"? That is what the Apostle Paul was talking about in Romans 6. *12 Let not sin therefore reign in your mortal body, to make you obey its passions. 13 Do not present your members to sin as instruments for unrighteousness, but present yourselves to God as those who have been brought from death to life, and your members to God as instruments for righteousness. 14 For sin will have no dominion over you, since you are not under law but under grace.* Romans 6:12-14 And in Romans 12:1 he tells us *to present your bodies as a living sacrifice, holy and acceptable to God, which is your spiritual worship.* Our total abandonment to God means it is no longer my way, but God's way. We vow by His grace to let Him have His way with our desires, thoughts, actions, speech, and goals.

18 Whoever rebels against your commandment and disobeys your words, whatever you command him, shall be put to death. Only be strong and courageous." Joshua 1:18 They declared their own punishment for desertion - death! That is ours as well, for if we desert the Lord, we will find the wages of sin is death (Romans 6:23). If we refuse His gracious gift of forgiveness, we will be insisting on paying our sin debt ourselves. That is more than physical death. It is called the second death (Revelation 2:11). And then they uttered a repetition of what Moses and the Lord had said to Joshua, "be strong and courageous." That is what they asked of him.

The many repetitions of this phrase lead me to believe that Joshua tended to be timid. Yet, he has led them through every battle on the way to the Promised Land. But then as we saw in a previous message, God often uses the weak to show it is His power and not man's strength. In that way He gets all the glory.

Our Joshua was strong and courageous to face the cross and the wrath of God on our sins for us. We don't have to wonder if the Lord will always be with Him, or if He will weaken, for He has already won the victory. We should follow Him into spiritual battle and even unto death, for He has defeated death itself. We have the Commander of the hosts of heaven with us (Joshua 4:14). We will meet Him in this book in chapter five (Joshua 5:15). Yes, Jesus appears to Joshua in a later chapter. If we will follow Him wherever He leads, we will be victorious in life and in death. If we are strong and courageous to do according all that He has told us, we too will spiritually prosper.

Will we trust and obey when the Word prompts us to action and the Spirit applies the Word to situations in our lives? Will we meditate on the Word day and night? Will we follow Jesus with courage, knowing the Lord is with us? Will we leave a spiritual legacy for our children? The alternative is to shrink back and stay where we are. That means we miss out on the land that God has for us to conquer. It is spiritual territory of abundant life in Christ and fellowship with Him.

If we settle for the land we have already taken and refuse to go forward following our Savior, we will wonder what might have been. Jesus tells us that whoever saves his or her life we will lose it. But if they lose their life for His sake, they will find it (Matthew 10:39). Take your eyes off the raging flood, the walled cities, and the giants of life's obstacles and turn them to Jesus, our mighty Captain (Hebrews 12:2). Be strong and courageous brothers and sisters, to follow Jesus wherever He leads. The Lord will be with you - and all that matters is that we are with Him.

Let us close this message with those of us who are willing vow to our Joshua what the people of Israel promised to their Joshua in verse 16: *"All that you have commanded us we will do, and wherever you send us we will go."* by the grace of God. Amen! If you mean it, say it with me.

Questions:
1 What is the promise to those who meditate on God's Word?
2 Why was God's command to Joshua daunting?
3 What flood did Jesus face?
4 What were they leaving behind?
5 What hardship did the 2 ½ tribes face? Why?
6 Why would they do that?
7 What is the "rest" written about in Hebrews?
8 Will you pray verse 16 to our Joshua?
9 Why was the penalty for disobedience so severe?
10 Will you leave a spiritual legacy for your posterity?
11 What are the benefits of doing so?

Providence and Faith Joshua 2

When Moses sent spies into the land almost forty years prior to this event, he sent one from each tribe, twelve spies. While they all agreed it was a fertile land only two said they should go in and take it, and that it was a land of milk and honey (Numbers 14:7,8). Milk and honey by the way means it was good for pastureland and crops. Milk comes from their herds and honey from the flowers of trees and plants. The ten naysayers were worried about the giants, an extremely tall race of people who lived in some of the cities.
32

¹ And Joshua the son of Nun sent two men secretly from Shittim as spies, saying, "Go, view the land, especially Jericho." And they went and came into the house of a prostitute whose name was Rahab and lodged there. Joshua 2:1 This time Joshua, who was one of the twelve that spied out the land the first time, chose only two loyal men of faith. He had learned that representatives and voting often went according to the fears of men. That is why the church today is to be led by elders who meet the qualifications in Titus and Timothy (Titus 1:5-9). Their lives show they are men of faith and will therefore operate in faith at God's leading in the Word instead of the whims of man.

He didn't announce their mission to avoid the possibility of a repeat of his past experience. The two men went into Jericho and stayed at a prostitute named Rahab's house. This does not mean they employed her services. Prostitutes' homes in that age were the local hotels. They had an extra room for their customers to stay.

² And it was told to the king of Jericho, "Behold, men of Israel have come here tonight to search out the land." Joshua 2:2 Someone noticed the two men and could probably tell by their dress and speech that they were Israelites. Since the huge company of Israelites were camped just across the Jordan, there would have been concern that they could be spies. The king was notified.

³ Then the king of Jericho sent to Rahab, saying, "Bring out the men who have come to you, who entered your house, for they have come to search out all the land." ⁴ But the woman had taken the two men and hidden them. And she said, "True, the men came to me, but I did not know where they were from. ⁵ Ands when the gate was about to be closed at dark, the men went out. I do not know where the men went. Pursue them quickly, for you will overtake them." Joshua 2:3-5 The king ordered that the men be brought out of Rahab's house. Rahab had hidden them. She lied, claiming she didn't know where they came from and that they left before dark. She suggested the king quickly make a search for them.

This brings up the issue of lying to protect someone. Sin is a serious matter, but some sins are more serious than others. Apostle Paul describes sexual sin is a more serious sin than some because it affects the body which is God's temple (1 Corinthians :18,19). Judaism teaches that when two commands conflict, we should consider which is weightier. Would it be more evil to lie or to turn the men over when it would mean their death? That would make her complicit in murder. In Nazi Germany, the Christians who hid Jews would lie to protect the lives of the Jews they were hiding. Should they have told the truth and watched them be taken to the camps to die?[v]

We rarely face this serious of a conflict, so we should never use the concept to justify having our way in a matter. There are times we must tell the truth even when it personally costs us a great deal. In the situation with Rahab, she was risking her life to protect the lives of the two men. Her lie could have had her executed if they were found. She acted in faith and is commended for doing so in Hebrews 11:31.

[6] But she had brought them up to the roof and hid them with the stalks of flax that she had laid in order on the roof. [7] So the men pursued after them on the way to the Jordan as far as the fords. And the gate was shut as soon as the pursuers had gone out. Joshua 2:6,7 Rooftops were a good place to dry grain. She hid the two men under the piled-up stalks of grain and then helped them escape after the search was over, by letting them down by rope out of her window. She would later hang a red cord in that window to identify her home when the Israelite army came. Centuries later The Apostle Paul would use the same

escape tactic to flee a trap set for him in Damascus (Acts 9:23-25). The men of Jericho went after them all the way to the Jordan River, which is only about a mile from the ancient city.

⁸ Before the men lay down, she came up to them on the roof ⁹ and said to the men, "I know that the LORD has given you the land, and that the fear of you has fallen upon us, and that all the inhabitants of the land melt away before you. ¹⁰ For we have heard how the LORD dried up the water of the Red Sea before you when you came out of Egypt, and what you did to the two kings of the Amorites who were beyond the Jordan, to Sihon and Og, whom you devoted to destruction. ¹¹ And as soon as we heard it, our hearts melted, and there was no spirit left in any man because of you, for the LORD your God, he is God in the heavens above and on the earth beneath. Joshua 2:8-11 Before hiding the men, Rahab made a deal with them. She told them that the people in Canaan had heard how God had led the Israelites to cross the Red Sea and parted the waters for them, as well as the defeat of the Amorite kings, Sihon and Og. She made a confession of faith that the God of Israel was the God of the heavens above and the earth beneath.

Because of the evil in those cultures, God instructed the Israelites to devote certain cities to destruction. That meant everything would be destroyed and everyone would die. Nothing could remain. This also put fear into the people of Canaan. Their hearts melted. They knew the God of the Israelites was God of heaven and earth, which means there is no place that can escape His justice. And still, they chose to resist Him.

We must stop here to explain what seems to be barbaric to us. It is one of the Bible critics' main arguments against the Bible. How could a loving God wipe out a culture? To understand this, we must look back to the time of Abraham. God promised Abraham that he would inherit the land but told him that first the iniquity of the people must come to the full (Genesis 15:16). That would be four hundred years later. In other words, over the next four centuries, God knew the wickedness of the people of the land would become like those people before the flood who only thought of evil continually (Genesis 6:5). Their religious ceremonies were orgies. Their sacrifices were their own children. Massive fields of sacrificed babies in ceramic jars have been discovered by archeologists.

The other factor we must consider is that the nation of Israel was a theocracy. God was making a judgment. Only God can say when a people group is so wicked that annihilation is the only solution before they corrupt other people. Israel was the only true theocracy in history. Genocide today is only done out of greed. We cannot compare the judgments of God with those of man, for God knows every detail of every heart. Man knows next to nothing in comparison. Devoting a city to destruction was obviously not for personal gain. When someone tried to make it so in the account of the conquest of Jericho, God judged that person (Joshua 7:25). That is because it sent a mixed message. The people were being destroyed because of the gravity of their sinful culture, not for any personal gain. It was also a warning to Israel that this could be their fate if they turned to the same evil practices.

I would like to point out the effect of the testimony of God in a person's life. No missionary came from Israel and witnessed to Jericho of what God had done. The news was carried by others. Your godly life can influence those whom you have never met. I often tell testimonies of people I never met. Their faithful, godly lives and what God accomplished through their prayers and service testify that God is God in heaven and earth. Every believer's life should testify to that fact.

At the same time, God saw one family, in the entire city that had faith in the God of Israel. It was certainly not who we would have chosen, but God sees the heart (1 Samuel 16:7). Everyone else in Jericho heard the same news but decided to try to resist God. He sovereignly sent the two spies to the house of that person of faith. She made her confession of faith. She risked her life for that faith, believing that the only way to save herself and her family was to side with God's people. What a picture of grace! What a picture of faith in action! She is commended two times in the New Testament for acting on her faith (James 2:25; Hebrews 11:31). Even more importantly, she ended up in the genealogy of the Messiah (Matthew 1:5)!

There within a city of pagans prepared to fight Israel's God was a prostitute who upon hearing the testimony of Israel began to have faith in God. The people of that time and place were pantheists. They believed there were gods over certain areas. How could God save her? With God all things are possible (Matthew 19:26). We can never guess who among our family and friends will turn to faith in Jesus. It is often the most unlikely ones. If God can reach into this pagan city and save one family, he can save anyone! That includes you and me. He is looking for people who will by faith place their trust in Him regardless of how they have lived to that point in their lives.

12 Now then, please swear to me by the LORD that, as I have dealt kindly with you, you also will deal kindly with my father's house, and give me a sure sign 13 that you will save alive my father and mother, my brothers and sisters, and all who belong to them, and deliver our lives from death." Joshua 2:12,13 Rahab wanted the spies to promise to save her and her family. As we read on, we find that the whole family must take shelter in her home to be saved. That would look suspicious. And why weren't the men required to be ready to battle against Israel? Somehow on that last day, the entire family barricaded themselves inside her home. That meant that they too were placing their faith in Israel's God. After all, to that point there had been no battles, just marching around the walls. So, we can see it was indeed faith in the God of Israel, not Israel's military might or war machines. Was it Rahab's faith that encouraged the family to believe? And when she told them the plan, she had to have faith that none of them would betray her to the king.

14 And the men said to her, "Our life for yours even to death! If you do not tell this business of ours, then when the LORD gives us the land we will deal kindly and faithfully with you." 15 Then she let them down by a rope through the window, for her house was built into the city wall, so that she lived in the wall. Joshua 2:14,15 The spies promised that if she died, they too would die. They promised to deal kindly and faithfully with her, as long as she did not tell their whereabouts. Kindness and faithfulness are the two most commonly mentioned attributes of God (*emet* and *hesed* Psalm 25:10). In other words, they would deal with her as God had dealt with them. The agreement now sealed with an oath, she let them down by a rope through the window. I have always referred to it as "the over the wall in a basket trick." She probably waited until nightfall so that darkness might hide their descent. If she was caught doing this, she would surely be executed. This action was putting her life into the hands of Israel's God.

16 And she said to them, "Go into the hills, or the pursuers will encounter you, and hide there three days until the pursuers have returned. Then afterward you may go your way." 17 The men said to her, "We will be guiltless with respect to this oath of yours that you have made us swear. Joshua 2:16,17 Rahab even suggested the best way for them to avoid capture. Instead of taking the road, she told them to go into the hills and wait for three days. Then they could return to the Israelite camp on the other side of Jordan. Joshua had given the people three days to prepare to cross. Her suggestion lined up with God's timing.

The hills around Jericho are the opposite direction from where they needed to go. It was a good strategy. Nearby was what is called the Mount of Temptation. The cliffs there have many caves, some of which are monasteries today.

18 Behold, when we come into the land, you shall tie this scarlet cord in the window through which you let us down, and you shall gather into your house your father and mother, your brothers, and all your father's household. 19 Then if anyone goes out of the doors of your house into the street, his blood shall be on his own head, and we shall be guiltless. But if a hand is laid on anyone who is with you in the house, his blood shall be on our head. 20 But if you tell this business of ours, then we shall be guiltless with respect to your oath that you have made us swear." Joshua 2:18-20 The oath for protection had three qualifications. Her family had to be inside her home, and she had to hang a scarlet cord in her window. It reminds us of the blood on the doorposts during the last plague in Egypt in which the family was to stay inside their house until the plague passed over. Perhaps that was what was on the spies' minds. The final qualification was that she could not tell anyone about them, or the oath would be voided.

21 And she said, "According to your words, so be it." Then she sent them away, and they departed. And she tied the scarlet cord in the window. Joshua 2:21 Rahab agreed to the deal. Then in faith she tied the scarlet cord in her window. It is interesting that it is scarlet. That may have been chosen because the die was expensive and it was unlikely anyone else would have had that color hanging from their window. But perhaps it was God's design to look forward to the blood of Christ that makes possible the salvation or our souls through faith.

When we hosted the Masterpiece Christian Art show, we had one painting that had angels looking down on the earth from a heavenly balcony. Over the railing hung a red sash that dropped down toward the earth representing salvation through faith in the blood shed for us. Come into the house of God with your whole family and shut the door behind you until judgement passes over (Exodus 12:22,23), which is exactly what the Jews did in Egypt. There is a scarlet cord of symbolism that runs throughout the Old Testament.

22 They departed and went into the hills and remained there three days until the pursuers returned, and the pursuers searched all along the way and found nothing. 23 Then the two men returned. They came down from the hills and passed over and came to Joshua the son of Nun, and they told him all that had happened to them. Joshua 2:22,23 The men followed her suggestion. The search party looked in the wrong direction as "all along the way" would have meant toward the Jordan. After three days - wait, I've heard that expression before. Now think of this. If they were hiding in a cave, then after three days they come out and cross the Jordan, which is a picture of death, only they are crossing in the opposite direction, would that not picture resurrection? Red chord, three days in the earth, and crossing back over Jordan! I think it is too much of a coincidence. It makes me wonder if this was one of the things Jesus shared on the road to Emmaus (Luke 24:44). Skeptics would say I see Jesus in everything. Amen! May it be so!

24 And they said to Joshua, "Truly the LORD has given all the land into our hands. And also, all the inhabitants of the land melt away because of us." Joshua

2:24 Just like the faithful two spies, Joshua and Caleb (Numbers 14:30), these two men report that the LORD has gone before them and put the fear of Him in the hearts of the inhabitants of the land. They see them already melting away because of God's prevenient grace. The providence of God had taken them to the only family of faith in the whole town. And Providence seeks throughout the whole earth to find the hearts that will open to His light and life (2 Chronicles 16:9a).

Our Joshua has gone before us through this life. He has written our days in His book before one of them came to be (Psalm 139:16). He has planned good works in advance for us to do (Ephesians 2:10). Let us be strong and very courageous to meditate on God's words day and night for then we too will be successful (Joshua 1:8), for the Lord will finish the work He has started in us (Philippians 1:6)! The enemy of our soul melts away before Him. His victory is ours as well for we are in Him.

Looking back over this account we see the hand of Providence guiding both the spies and Rahab. We see their mutual faith trusting in the circumstances God had orchestrated. A thousand things could have gone wrong. They could have been found in the flax on the roof or spotted going down the wall. One of Rahab's family members could have lacked faith and spoiled the whole plan. Our minds can come up with every possible scenario for failure, but faith believes in the providence of God. Faith sees what God has done in the past and trusts Him for the present circumstances and future as well.

When we put our faith in Christ Jesus, we enter the spiritual land Jesus called the kingdom of God (Matthew 21:31). Circumstances test our conviction that the whole land of that kingdom of God is indeed ours. We see the enemies of the world, our old nature, and the devil and his demons at work. But brothers and sisters, the battle is already won. Our Joshua is already victorious (Matthew 28:18). Those hindrances we see will be gone forever. His Word promises it is so. The providences of God in our lives reminds us it is true. *Truly the Lord has given all the land into our hands!* Hallelujah!

Questions:
1 Why were only two spies sent?
2 Why is Rahab's lie seen as faith?
3 Why might the red scarf be significant?
4 What influenced Rahab to convert?
5 Why is God's dealing through Israel different from how He works in nations today?
6 Why did God demand the destruction of the city?
7 In what ways did Rahab express faith?
8 In what ways did the spies express faith?
9 What part did providence play in this account?
10 How can we apply this account to our lives?

He Goes Before Joshua 3

[1] Then Joshua rose early in the morning and they set out from Shittim. And they came to the Jordan, he and all the people of Israel, and lodged there before they passed over. Joshua 3:1 While the spies were hiding in the hills to west of Jericho, the camp of Israel moved to the edge of the Jordan and prepared to cross (if the three days of hiding corresponds to the three days the officers waited to go through the camp). Joshua was up early the morning they were to move. No doubt he was full of anticipation and maybe a bit nervous. The Jordan is at flood stage and the imposing walls of Jericho could be seen in the distance. But the promises of God to give them the land have led to this point. He told the people the last time they came to this spot that the Lord was surely able to give them the land.

42

Now here they are again, but Moses is dead. However, the God of Moses is not dead. He is the One whodirected Moses and gave them victories.

² At the end of three days the officers went through the camp ³ and commanded the people, "As soon as you see the ark of the covenant of the LORD your God being carried by the Levitical priests, then you shall set out from your place and follow it. ⁴ Yet there shall be a distance between you and it, about 2,000 cubits in length. Do not come near it, in order that you may know the way you shall go, for you have not passed this way before." Joshua 3:2-4 It was time to move out. The people had heard the promises and knew of their parents' failures. By now they had the encouraging word from the returning spies. But they could see what Joshua saw. In front of them was a raging river at least ten feet deep, and with them are children and flocks. Now the moment has come. What would happen? What would God do?

The officers informed the people to follow the ark of the covenant. The excitement must have been tangible. They were to keep a safe distance of 3000 feet behind it. The ark was the symbol of the presence of God with them. They had never come this way before. Those who dared to try to go in without God died in the wilderness. But now God goes before them just as He has all the way through the wilderness as a pillar of cloud by day and fire by night.

This is a lesson to us on how God builds our faith. He puts us in impossible situations and tells us to go forward. He assures us that He is with us (Matthew 28:20). All we need to do is follow Him like they followed the ark. The big difference is that while we revere His holiness, we are invited to draw near (Hebrews 4:16). We don't need to stay at a distance. Jesus' righteousness covers us as we approach God.

We have no idea how He will see us through or what He will do in the process. We just have to have faith and obey (Isaiah 50:10). And when we do, we often find this way we have never been before turns out in ways we could never have imagined. When we walk by faith instead of by sight, we then see the wonders of God (2 Corinthians 5:7). It is uncomfortable as we begin, but looking back, we see God has gone before us and made a way.

It is not our role to second-guess what God will do, any more than it is to argue about how he could possibly do it. We have to follow. Faith gathers up all our cares and anxieties in the knowledge that He has taken the responsibility for our future and every step ahead of us. Faith leaves it all with God (see Psalm 55:22; 1 Peter 5:7).[vi]

As soon as they cross the Jordan, everything will change. The cloud will be gone. The manna will stop falling. They will be in the Promised Land and it will supply their needs. But one thing will not have changed. They are still following the LORD, now represented by the ark of the covenant.

[5] *Then Joshua said to the people, "Consecrate yourselves, for tomorrow the LORD will do wonders among you."* Joshua 3:5 The day before the departure they were to consecrate themselves, which meant to wash their clothing and prepare their hearts (Exodus 19:10). This was what their parents did when they made a covenant with God on Sinai. This was a careful and deliberate preparation for a profound moment in the history of the nation. The promise to Abraham was about to take a step toward fulfillment. God was about to do something they would never forget, and they needed to be ready to take it in.

In Kent Hughes book on the *Disciplines of a Godly Man*, he suggests that we do a similar kind of preparation for our time of worship together on Sunday. He suggests that we do all the preparation the night before, such as laying out our clothes and getting to bed on time so we will not be rushed in the morning. I would also suggest reading the passage for that Sunday if you are aware of it. Then come that morning with an expectation to encounter God in His Word. Prepare your heart beforehand with prayer. If we want to see His wonders, we need to consecrate ourselves beforehand lest we take the wonders of God lightly or miss them altogether.

6 And Joshua said to the priests, "Take up the ark of the covenant and pass on before the people." So they took up the ark of the covenant and went before the people. Joshua 3:6 The time had come. The priests put their shoulders under the rods that carried the ark and began to move out. They were acting in faith that God did speak to Joshua, as we will see in the following verses. They were about to carry the ark into a flood, but they obeyed. The people could see that God was going before them to make a way through the Jordan.

As the Jordan is a picture of death, we should realize that our Savior has gone before us to make a way through death. He crossed over and rose victorious. Because He lives, we will live also (John 14:19). When our day comes to cross the Jordan, we can cross over without fear for God has gone before us and made a way (John 14:6).

7 The LORD said to Joshua, "Today I will begin to exalt you in the sight of all Israel, that they may know that, as I was with Moses, so I will be with you. Joshua 3:7 Verses 7 through 13 appear to be God's instructions to Joshua and Joshua passing on those instructions to the people. God's purpose in bringing them to the Jordan during the annual flood was to help them place their faith in Joshua like they had trusted in Moses. Did he hear from God as Moses did? Was his leading at the command of

God? This miracle would put an end to those questions and give them faith to obey him in the upcoming battles.

We need to understand that Joshua was a foreshadow of Jesus. These divinely appointed and anointed leaders in the Old Testament, such as kings and prophets, had the Spirit of God come upon them for their ministry. People were to obey them without question unless they were encouraging the worship of other gods. The change that came about in the New Testament is that every child of God has the Spirit within them.

The wisdom of God in the New Testament instructs us to have multiple elders rather than a single leader (Titus 1:5). They consult God's Word, listen to one another and pray over issues. They keep one another accountable. They support one another through difficulties and share the burden of watching over the flock. It keeps a sincere godly leader from burning out. They have a diversity of gifts. Hebrews 13:17 tells us to submit to their leadership. But we also have the injunction that we ought to obey God rather than man (Acts 5:29). We each have the Spirit of God in us and the Word of God in our hands. Our Joshua is Jesus, and He alone is the head of the church (Ephesians 1:22).

⁸ And as for you, command the priests who bear the ark of the covenant, 'When you come to the brink of the waters of the Jordan, you shall stand still in the Jordan.'" ⁹ And Joshua said to the people of Israel, "Come here and listen to the words of the LORD your God." ¹⁰ And Joshua said, "Here is how you shall know that the living God is among you and that he will without fail drive out from before you the Canaanites, the Hittites, the Hivites, the Perizzites, the Girgashites, the Amorites, and the Jebusites. Joshua 3:8-10 God gave Joshua specific instructions for the priests and for the people. The priests were to carry the ark into the Jordan and stand still. Since the people could only come within 3000 foot of the ark, the priests would have been upstream over half a mile from the people.

Then Joshua called the people to listen to the words of the Lord. That is what we do every time we open the Bible. God's instructions were to serve the explicit purpose of assuring them that God was with them to drive out the nations that lived in the Promised Land.

The spiritual parallel is that the miracle God did in saving our souls is a sign to you that He goes before you to drive out all the obstacles that keep you from entering into kingdom living: impure thoughts, fear, the patterns of pleasure in sin, and the selfish way we lived our lives. These are our flood waters. They are also the enemies in our land, and they look too powerful for us to overcome, but God goes before us. He is the One who will rewire our thought life if we will follow Him and live in His Word (Romans 12:2). He will replace our destructive temporal pleasures with greater and more fulfilling and lasting ones. He will be the spirit of selflessness in us as we surrender our will to His. He goes before us, brothers and sisters. We do make an effort to see these changes come about in our mind and heart (2 Peter 1:5), but it is by His enabling power and grace that dries up our Jordan.

11 Behold, the ark of the covenant of the Lord of all the earth is passing over before you into the Jordan.
12 Now therefore take twelve men from the tribes of Israel, from each tribe a man. 13 And when the soles of the feet of the priests bearing the ark of the LORD, the Lord of all the earth, shall rest in the waters of the Jordan, the waters of the Jordan shall be cut off from flowing, and the waters coming down from above shall stand in one heap." Joshua 3:11-13 Surely God had explained all this to Joshua, so what we have in verses 7 and 8 are just summary of what God said. Now we have the details. They were to appoint a man from each tribe. We will see the purpose in the

following verses. When the priests' feet touched the Jordan River, God would cause the water to stop flowing and pile up. It was as if a giant invisible hand was going to come down and make an enormous dam.

Think of the faith it took Joshua to declare that to the people! If the soles of the priest's feet touched the water and nothing happened, what do you think they would have done to Joshua? Joshua told the people what God commanded him to say, so the burden is not on Joshua but on God. The same is true when we believe the Word of God.

A problem we have in this age is people speaking for God things that never come about. They say, "God told me to tell you so and so ..." When it doesn't happen, they do not reevaluate their ability to hear and discern the voice of God, they just carry on as if God goofed. God doesn't promise and then fail to fulfill. Compare these proclamations from people to the Word of God and the sense the Holy Spirit gives you in your spirit. If you are living in the Spirit and know God's Word, you will have an immediate sense whether or not the person is in tune with God.

[14] So when the people set out from their tents to pass over the Jordan with the priests bearing the ark of the covenant before the people, [15] and as soon as those bearing the ark had come as far as the Jordan, and the feet of the priests bearing the ark were dipped in the brink of the water (now the Jordan overflows all its banks throughout the time of harvest), [16] the waters coming down from above stood and rose up in a heap very far away, at Adam, the city that is beside Zarethan, and those flowing down toward the Sea of the Arabah, the Salt Sea, were completely cut off. And the people passed over opposite Jericho. Joshua 3:14-16 Faith and obedience will overcome any obstacle no matter how great. Can you see

the priests with the ark approaching the banks of the river now flooding the plain? I live on a creek that has steep banks, so I always imagined them stepping off an embankment. Recently we discovered where the excavation for Bethsaida was on the north shore of Galilee. We took a group there in the springtime, but it was impossible to approach because the Jordan had overflowed its banks into the surrounding farmland making the approach a mud bog. That gave me a clearer picture of what it would have been like. They would have been stepping into shallow muddy water first and then come to the main channel. But as soon as the soles of their feet touched the water, the Jordan stopped flowing. What is just as amazing is that in the next verse we read the ground was dry!

The nation had heard of the amazing crossing of the Red Sea. Moses had stretched out his staff and the sea parted, and the people went across on dry ground. If there was any miracle that would have helped people see that God was with Joshua like he was with Moses, the parting of the water was it! The invisible hand of God came down and made a dam near a city called Adam. God has a sense of humor: A-dam!

17 Now the priests bearing the ark of the covenant of the LORD stood firmly on dry ground in the midst of the Jordan, and all Israel was passing over on dry ground until all the nation finished passing over the Jordan. Joshua 3:17 The priests stood there in the middle of the riverbed until the whole nation passed over. That was another act of faith. It would have taken all day for the nation to cross over with their children and herds.

One day the creek we live on was at flood stage. We heard a great roar and the ground shook. Our neighbor on the creek called and said the flood was almost up to his window. A landslide had instantly created a dam. The creek below stopped flowing. But once the water began to break through, that pent up water became a flashflood. When the ocean shore or a water way goes dry, run the other way. It will come back with a vengeance. The Israelites knew this as they had surely seen flashfloods in the wadis of the wilderness they lived in for the past 40 years.

I think the priests felt perfectly safe because they were with the ark of the covenant. They were with the object where the presence of God manifested Himself. They had seen His wonders and knew He was indeed God in heaven above and earth below (Joshua 2:11). They were in the safest place in all the world.

The entire nation passed over to the side where the city of Jericho was. The manna would now stop. The cloud that led them now lifted. They were home. Well, they were almost home. There was a little matter of the nations still in their land. But if God can stop a flooding river, what are the armies of man? The wonder of the miracle would stay with them the rest of their lives. If their fathers were baptized into Moses in the Red Sea, they were now baptized into Joshua in the Jordan (1 Corinthians 10:1,2).

It is tempting to take this account and draw a sweeping conclusion that God will remove every obstacle in our way. But that is a self-centered application that is not consistent with the whole account. What is clear is that God keeps His promises. Nothing can stop His Word from being fulfilled, for it was by His Word that all things were created (Psalm 33:9). The Israelites had faced many problems in the wilderness, some were the consequences of their sins, and others came from the sins of other nations. Nevertheless, God has kept His promise to bring them into the land. They will face many more problems in the conquest for the same reasons. But God is with them. And through them, God was bringing His Word into the world, both the written and incarnate Word. He was constantly pointing to the coming Messiah through their history. In the end, we will find it was all about Jesus and the glory of God (Luke 24:27).

It is Jesus who stood in the Jordan, the symbol of death, so that we might enter the promised land of the kingdom of God, not someday when we die, but right now (Romans 8:11). He stopped the flood of our fallen nature by His grace and invited us in (Ephesians 2:8,9). We have received the Spirit but still our flesh is at war with our spirit, and we have much land to conquer (Galatians 5:17). But if we will take the key principle here, which is to trust God and His promises, then we will find He leads us to many victories and provides our needs as well. We will conquer spiritual land that we will leave as a heritage for our children, for the miracle working God who stopped the Jordan is working in our lives as well, bringing us into our promised land of life in Christ. The Apostle Paul tells us that He who began a good work in us will be faithful to complete it (Philippians 1:6). Our lives will be increasingly conformed into the likeness of Jesus (Romans 8:29) and point others to our Savior. We will find it was all for the glory of our great God.

Questions:
1 How daunting was the command from God?
2 What lesson should we learn from that?
3 Why is the Jackman quote a struggle to live out?
4 What was the purpose of God's command?
5 Would you have told the people what God told Joshua?
6 What was as big a miracle as the water stopping?
7 Why would it still take faith to cross?
8 What was their assurance?
9 Does God remove all our obstacles?

10 Who stopped our flood? Is He your assurance of everlasting life?

Memorial Stones Joshua 4:1-5:1

In the previous chapter the Lord had told the people that when they saw God dry up the Jordan River, they would know that God would defeat the nations on the other side of the Jordan. It was a sign to give them confidence in the Lord's power and in Joshua as their leader. It was proof that Joshua was hearing from the Lord.

¹ When all the nation had finished passing over the Jordan, the LORD said to Joshua, ² "Take twelve men from the people, from each tribe a man, ³and command them, saying, 'Take twelve stones from here out of the midst of the Jordan, from the very place where the priests' feet stood firmly, and bring them over with you and lay them down in the place where you lodge tonight.'" ⁴ Then Joshua called the twelve men from the people of Israel, whom he had appointed, a man from each tribe. ⁵And Joshua said to them, "Pass on before the ark of the LORD your God into the midst of the Jordan, and take up each of you a stone upon his shoulder, according to the number of the tribes of the people of Israel, Joshua 4:1-5

The nation had passed over with their families and herds and the tabernacle of God. What do you think the people of Jericho thought when they saw this took place? If Tel Jericho is the ancient site of Jericho, the people of Jericho could have watched that event. Spies surely witnessed it. What chance do you have against an army whose God stops a river for them? The smart move would have been to wave the white flag and say, "Here is our city, we give it to you, just tell us about your God so we can worship Him." The fact that they did not do so is evidence of the hardness of their hearts.

In chapter 3 the LORD commanded Joshua to pick a man from each tribe. It does not tell us the purpose until we get to these verses. They were to go into the dry riverbed and pick out twelve stones from where the priests were standing and bring them into the camp. They could not have been very large stones, as each man carried the stone on his shoulder. They were to bring them to the place they would camp, Gilgal.

⁶ that this may be a sign among you. When your children ask in time to come, 'What do those stones mean to you?' ⁷ then you shall tell them that the waters of the Jordan were cut off before the ark of the covenant of the LORD. When it passed over the Jordan, the waters of the Jordan were cut off. So these stones shall be to the people of Israel a memorial forever." Joshua 4:6,7 In those days people would stand large stones to mark important events and remind future generations of what had taken place (1 Samuel 7:12). Sometimes the stones would bear inscriptions explaining the event or treaty. This pile of twelve stones was to remind the future Israelites of the miracle that God did in opening the way into the land He had promised to Abraham's descendants (Genesis 17:8). God had shown His amazing power in parting the Red Sea to deliver them from the Egyptians (Exodus 14:21), and now in a similar way He parted the Jordan and dried up the passageway so the Israelites could enter the Promised Land. Both ends of the wilderness journey were marked by a parting of the waters.

The Bible begins with a parting of the waters. Genesis 1:6 tells us God separated the waters from the waters. In Revelation 17:15 we are told that waters are representative of people. Could it be that God was emphasizing the fact that He was separating them to be a people for Himself both in coming out of Egypt and in entering the Promised Land to conquer the nations? Listen to the instruction of 2 Corinthians 6:17,18. *17 Therefore go out from their midst, and be separate from them, says the Lord, and touch no unclean thing; then I will welcome you, 18 and I will be a father to you, and you shall be sons and daughters to me, says the Lord Almighty."* God has always been seeking a people to call His sons and daughters (Isaiah 43:6). He calls us out of the world's nations and makes us a nation of kings and priests (Exodus 19:6).

We don't know where that pile of stones is today, but stones don't just vanish. They are probably still in the area, buried with the sands of time. The historical fact that the entire nation crossed over when the Jordan was overflowing its banks stands as a testimony to the faithfulness of God to keep His promises. What has remained for all to read is the account we are reading, preserved by God despite all the attempts throughout history to destroy it. It is a miracle that these Scriptures survived. In that sense our Bibles are the standing stones that remain.

It is also a miracle that there is still a nation of Israel to be reminded of God's faithfulness. Nations don't disappear for 2000 years and suddenly reemerge without God intervening. Both the Scriptures and the existence of the nation of Israel remind us of the faithfulness of our God (Deuteronomy 7:9)!

There is a stone that we look to today. Jesus went through the great flood of the wrath of God, and God carried Him out and established the memorials of communion and baptism. Those memorials remind us of His great acts of death for our sins, burial, and resurrection. Our Cornerstone is also the capstone (Isaiah 28:16), the beginning and the end (Revelation 21:6). We are to be reminded regularly and to tell our children that God made a way for us (Deuteronomy 6:7). Just as the ark of the covenant representing the presence of God stopped the flood waters, so our Savior stood in the way of the wrath of God, and in doing so He made a way for us to pass over from death to life.

⁸ And the people of Israel did just as Joshua commanded and took up twelve stones out of the midst of the Jordan, according to the number of the tribes of the people of Israel, just as the LORD told Joshua. And they carried them over with them to the place where they lodged and laid them down there. ⁹ And Joshua set up twelve stones in the midst of the Jordan, in the place where the feet of the priests bearing the ark of the covenant had stood; and they are there to this day. Joshua 4:8,9 There is an expression repeated ten times in Joshua, "just as the LORD (or Moses or Joshua) commanded." This is emphasizing the faithfulness of Joshua and the people of Israel during this time in their history. While the people will have short periods of history where they turn to the LORD, they are soon followed by a period of unfaithfulness. The repetition of the expression is emphasizing Joshua's faithfulness as a leader. In that sense he foreshadows our leader, Yeshua/Jesus, the ultimate leader who gives us the power of the Holy Spirit to enable us to faithfully follow (Acts 1:8).

Verse eight describes the twelve men carrying out Joshua's command to set up the stones at their camp. There is a difference of opinion about the original language of verse nine. It is either describing Joshua setting up the stones the men took from the Jordan, or describing Joshua erecting twelve stones in the Jordan riverbed. The Israelites had experience moving large stones from their time in Egypt. They may have set up such large stones in the riverbed that flood waters did not move them.

¹⁰ For the priests bearing the ark stood in the midst of the Jordan until everything was finished that the LORD commanded Joshua to tell the people, according to all that

Moses had commanded Joshua. The people passed over in haste. ¹¹ And when all the people had finished passing over, the ark of the LORD and the priests passed over before the people. ¹² The sons of Reuben and the sons of Gad and the half-tribe of Manasseh passed over armed before the people of Israel, as Moses had told them. ¹³ About 40,000 ready for war passed over before the LORD for battle, to the plains of Jericho. ¹⁴ On that day the LORD exalted Joshua in the sight of all Israel, and they stood in awe of him just as they had stood in awe of Moses, all the days of his life. Joshua 4:10-14

While the presence of God represented by the ark of the Lord was in the riverbed, the priests knew they were safe. The people went over in haste as it would take all day even if they were 100 abreast. The men whose families remained on the other side came just as they had promised Moses. We are given the number of men aged twenty probably to fifty years of age (Numbers 4:3) from two and a half tribes, 40,000. That is about 16,000 per tribe, which times twelve would be an army of about 192,000 soldiers.

One purpose of God in this event was to have the people be in awe of Joshua like they had been in awe of Moses. Joshua was the appointed leader of the theocracy, and in unity with the high priest, Eleazar, they heard from God and faithfully relayed His instructions to the people. Remember it was Joshua who often remained at the tent of meeting even after Moses finished speaking with the LORD (Exodus 33:11).

As I have pointed out earlier, we now have the Word of God in written form, the full revelation of God. We have the record of the life of Jesus who revealed God to us (Hebrews 1:1-3). Believers have the Holy Spirit residing in them (Ephesians 2:22). The church is not a theocratic nation, but rather Spirit led individuals in groups led by the Word and equal and accountable elders

(Hebrews 13:17). And yet, together with those who have gone before, we make up the body of Christ, the kingdom of God.

I can say that I have been in awe of a few men of God who demonstrated the fruits of the Spirit and lived lives of total dedication. Not one of them ever tried to tell me what God's will was for me. In fact, the people who did try I generally saw as misguided. We have too many church leaders who would like to hold this kind of Old Testament authority. They say, "Thus saith the Lord!" But when it doesn't come to pass, people still continue to follow them. Church, use discernment. Learn to sense that check in your heart from the Spirit (Isaiah 30:21). If you walk with the Lord each day and get to know God's Word, you won't be intimidated or misled by these charlatans who claim to speak for God. You will instead quote to them the Scriptures which contradict their babble.

There is an exception to this. Sometimes a brother or sister will share a verse with you out of a humble heart and that verse convicts you. You know in your spirit that it was from God. They don't have to say, "God told me to tell you..." You will know. It will come in the spirit of love (1 Corinthians 14:3). That is a blessing (Proverbs 27:6)!

15 And the LORD said to Joshua, 16 "Command the priests bearing the ark of the testimony to come up out of the Jordan." 17 So Joshua commanded the priests, "Come up out of the Jordan." 18 And when the priests bearing the ark of the covenant of the LORD came up from the midst of the Jordan, and the soles of the priests' feet were lifted up on dry ground, the waters of the Jordan returned to their place and overflowed all its banks, as before. Joshua 4:15-18 I would have expected a huge wall of water to have come roaring down the riverbed once the water was released, but it appears God let it out slowly so it simply returned to the normal flood level. Remember the people of Jericho could see all this from the top of their walls.

¹⁹ The people came up out of the Jordan on the tenth day of the first month, and they encamped at Gilgal on the east border of Jericho. ²⁰ And those twelve stones, which they took out of the Jordan, Joshua set up at Gilgal. ²¹ And he said to the people of Israel, "When your children ask their fathers in times to come, 'What do these stones mean?' ²² then you shall let your children know, 'Israel passed over this Jordan on dry ground.'²³ For the LORD your God dried up the waters of the Jordan for you until you passed over, as the LORD your God did to the Red Sea, which he dried up for us until we passed over, Joshua 4:19-23 The tenth of Nisan was the day in which Israelites were to select their lamb for the Passover on the 14th. Then they left Egypt to follow the cloud to the Promised Land (Exodus 12:3,6). Their entry into the Promised Land of milk and honey was a new beginning also. But there was another event that happened centuries later on the tenth of Nisan, the Triumphal Entry (Matthew 21:6-9), when Jesus presented Himself to be the sacrificial Lamb of God (John 1:29). The fact that God had Jesus enter Jerusalem on that date is to show that the event pictured new beginnings, liberation, and inheritance. Jesus' sacrifice of Himself brings us out of bondage (John 8:34) and wilderness wandering and into the promised land of eternal life filled with the fruits of the Spirit (Galatians 5:22,23).

Gilgal, we find in the next chapter, means rolled away. The reproach of the people was rolled away. We will talk about that important point in the next chapter. It was there that Joshua set up the twelve stones taken out of the Jordan. We have quite a bit of repetition in this chapter. That is for emphasis. It is important for us to tell our children and grandchildren the things God has done for us, the miracles He has done in our lives. If you are born-again, they need to know about that miracle.

We have seen miracles here at Wayside. We see God provide financially to give such a large portion of our income to missions each year and still have a fairly-compensated staff. Many churches our size struggle with that, but we never have. We have seen the conversion of New Age leaders and drug addicts. We have seen people commit their lives to a mission and give up everything to do so. We saw God challenge us to give $100,000 to missions and then replace it even before we gave it out. We have seen many lives that were lukewarm become dedicated to Jesus. We have seen thousands subscribe to the sermons from this little church and disciples made in foreign nations. Have you told your children and grandchildren? We certainly should.

One modern way of setting up standing stones is to have a diary of how God has worked in our lives. Leave it behind for posterity. And why do we do this? So that all the peoples of the earth may know that the hand of the LORD is mighty, and that you may fear/reverence the LORD your God forever!

24 so that all the peoples of the earth may know that the hand of the LORD is mighty, that you may fear the LORD your God forever." Joshua 4:24 Here are the two reasons God did this amazing miracle. The first is that the world might know that God is mighty. Israel was chosen by God to be a testimony to the world that our Creator is great, to be held in awe, and is reaching out to us (John 3:17). Israel was to be an evangelistic message to the world of the goodness and grace of God. But, like much of the church today, they began to see themselves as the chosen frozen and despise those who were not Jews. Their outreach was mostly for the reason of boasting and conforming others to their many rules. The same thing happens today with all faiths. Rules end up substituting for a genuine relationship that God desires.

Secondly, it was to cause the Jews to be in awe of God forever, to reverence His holiness and fear His judgments. Four times in this passage Joshua told them God is the LORD *your* God. He is a personal God who has claimed us as His own. We need to remember He is *our* Almighty God (Matthew 19:26).

Remembering is an important task of the followers of Jesus. We celebrate communion so that we might remember (Luke 22:19). In a world where we are constantly seeking new experiences, new information, and new technology, we can forget the greatness of God as recorded in His Word and even as experienced in our own lives. That is why remembering is important. Write down those amazing encounters with God, the coincidences that are just too strange to be an accident, where you saw God at work in your life. Remembering is why reading through the Bible is a necessity that should be a lifelong habit (Psalm 103:2).

More than the miracle, the emphasis is on the greatness of God. It was to encourage the people's faith in God. It also put the fear of God in the enemies and warning them that they were serving false gods. *[1] As soon as all the kings of the Amorites who were beyond the Jordan to the west, and all the kings of the Canaanites who were by the sea, heard that the LORD had dried up the waters of the Jordan for the people of Israel until they had crossed over, their hearts melted and there was no longer any spirit in them because of the people of Israel.* Joshua 5:1

This is the conclusion of the previous chapter. The Canaanites must have wondered what kind of people serve a God who would stop a raging river for them. They had already heard of their crossing of the Red Sea and the victories over the nations on the other side of the Jordan.

Who could stand against a people with a God like that? Surely, as Rahab declared, *"He is God in heaven above and the earth beneath"* (Joshua 2:11). He is the same God today! He is still doing wonders, and we need to hear and share those testimonies especially with our children and those with whom God put us together.

The fact that God did this in the sight of the people of Jericho also shows His gracious warnings to repent or perish (Luke 13:3). He had given that people group 400 years to repent and change their ways (Genesis 15:16), yet He still gave them one last visible warning. He does not desire the death of the wicked but invites the world to Himself in love while also warning of His justice (1 John 4:9,10).

The nation of Israel could rest without fear of attack that night for the God who does wonders had shown His power again. God's love expressed on the cross and His power in the resurrection is why we can rest secure in this life. We serve an all-powerful, holy, God.

Communion is our standing stone, our memorial marker, the place we go to remember the mighty acts of God. That is where we find our rest. It is a visible reminder so much greater than the twelves stones, for it points to the Cornerstone who is also the Capstone, and the Rock of offense (Isaiah 8:14). It tells us of how great God's love is for us (John 15:13). It reminds us of the great cost paid in love so that we, the children of God, could enter our promised land. The Son of God loved you and me and gave His life for us (Galatians 2:20). Have you entered His rest and ceased from your own labors (Hebrews 4:10)? Are you standing on that unshakable Rock of faith in Christ Jesus? Jesus taught that if we build our house on a rock it will stand the storms of life (Matthew 7:24,25). The only standing stone to build our life around is the rock of Christ Jesus, remembering all He accomplished for us.

Questions:
1 Why and how did God warn Jericho?
2 Why did they set up twelve stones?
3 What stone reminds us of God's great acts?
4 What is the difference between the church and Israel?
5 What events happened on the 10th of Nisan? Connection?
6 Why did God stop the Jordan River?
7 What is our act of remembrance?
8 Why was this the time to enter?
9 Why could they rest while in the sight of their enemy?
10 Why can we rest though Satan is a roaring lion?

No More Shame Joshua 5:2-12

To understand today's passage, we need to know some facts about the Hebrew culture and history. First, we should understand that the Hebrews saw the physical world as representation of spiritual realities. The Apostle Paul makes that point that was realized by his culture in the opening of his letter to the Romans. He tells us that the invisible things of God are clearly seen in the things that are made (Romans 1:20). He also reminds us that we should learn from the experiences of Israel (1 Corinthians 10:6).

Next, we need to know the background of circumcision. It was the sign of a covenant between God and Abraham and his descendants. The covenant promised that God would give them the land of Canaan (Genesis 17:8). They were to be to God as a nation of priests who followed His commands and who would love Him with their whole hearts (Exodus 19:5,6). Moses explained that circumcision was a sign of the covenant, an outward picture of an inward act. He told the children of Israel to circumcise their hearts (Deuteronomy 10:16). In other words, to be sensitive to God. It was to identify them as a people separated to God for His glory. This nation of diverse ethnicity was to be united in having a heart that was sensitive to God (Exodus 12:38).

After Moses led the new nation out of Egypt, they came to the Jordan River and sent spies into the land, one spy from each tribe. Ten of the spies discouraged the nation from trying to take the land because of the ferocity and size of the people living there. So the people said they would rather die in the wilderness (Numbers 14:2). For the next thirty-nine years the older generation did die out as they wandered through the wilderness. Now their children have entered the land. The battles had not yet begun.

² At that time the LORD said to Joshua, "Make flint knives and circumcise the sons of Israel a second time." ³ So Joshua made flint knives and circumcised the sons of Israel at Gibeath-haaraloth. ⁴ And this is the reason why Joshua circumcised them: all the males of the people who came out of Egypt, all the men of war, had died in the wilderness on the way after they had come out of Egypt. ⁵ Though all the people who came out had been circumcised, yet all the people who were born on the way in the wilderness after they had come out of Egypt had not been circumcised. Joshua 5:2-5 There is an important pattern in this book we might easily skip over. God tells Joshua to do something and then the text tells us he did it. It is repetitious for a reason. Joshua always obeys right away. This is another reason he is a foreshadow of the Messiah, Jesus. Jesus only did what He saw the Father doing. He only judged as the Father judged (John 5:19,30). He is our perfect example.

God told Joshua to make flint knives. Did you know that flint can be as sharp as surgical steel? God told him to use the least painful of tools. Then he got to work and circumcised all the men who were born during the wilderness journey. Those men who left Egypt were circumcised sometime before they left. We don't know if it was when they were born or if it was possibly a renewal of the covenant sometime before they left Egypt. That may be why the text says, "a second time."

This was a great act of faith on the part of the nation. It made them vulnerable. They surely knew the story of their ancestors who tricked a town into circumcising their men and then while they were in that weakened condition slaughtered them because their prince had abused their sister Dinah (Genesis 34). Now they were the ones in the weakened condition and within sight of the huge walls of Jericho. They knew that they could have been attacked. But what God ordered they obeyed.

Circumcision was the seal of the covenant God made with Abraham. You can read about it in Genesis 17. As they were about to launch the conquest of Canaan it was a reminder that the God of Abraham was their God and that He promised the whole land of Canaan as an everlasting possession to Abraham's descendants (Genesis 17:8). Four hundred years had passed, but now the promise was about to be fulfilled. If they wanted to see it fulfilled, they needed to keep their side of the covenant.

Circumcision was an outward sign of an inward change. Moses had told them to circumcise their hearts and not be stiff-necked. Today baptism represents a similar thing. It is a picture of dying, being buried, and raised to new life with Jesus (Romans 6:3,4). It symbolizes entrance into the New Covenant we make when we give our lives to Jesus and receive His life. We exchange our sins for His righteousness (2 Corinthians 5:21). Then we become the nation of priests that Israel was meant to foreshadow.

The men of Israel knew their fathers had died in the wilderness because they did not have faith in God and showed their lack of faith by their continual murmuring.

When their fathers had come to the Jordan River, they refused to trust God and go in. Now their descendants are in the same place, but they are trusting God to the point of even becoming vulnerable before their enemies. They put their complete trust in God.

We should notice that it wasn't because Joshua or the people said, "Hey, we haven't done what God told us do as a sign of the covenant between us and God. We need to be circumcised!" No, it was God who told Joshua they were forgetting an act of obedience. Compromise had to be dealt with before they moved forward. They needed to be right with God in every way before they began their campaign. God was about to deliver His side of the covenant and they needed to keep their side of it.

We too must see that we have buried our old life with Christ and been raised with Him before we move forward in the spiritual warfare we face (Colossians 2:11,12). If we are constantly complaining and rebelling like the older generation that died in the wilderness, we won't enter the land God has for us to take. Our enemies are not people, but the spiritual forces of darkness in the heavenly realms (Ephesians 6:12). Those forces would have us be fearful and discouraged so that we don't take the land but remain in the wilderness of life. They would have us give up and become satisfied with just knowing what Jesus did for us. But Jesus died to give us new life now, not some day in the future (Romans 8:11). He wants us to be soldiers of a spiritual nature who point others to the victorious life that can be ours in Jesus. He wants us to bear fruit that lasts (John 15:16), not take a little land and then let it be taken back. I am not talking about temporal things, the passing governments of this world, or political power. I'm talking about what will remain forever, the souls of men and women. Onward Christian soldiers claiming the spiritual land for our King!

6 or the people of Israel walked forty years in the wilderness, until all the nation, the men of war who came out of Egypt, perished, because they did not obey the voice of the LORD; the LORD swore to them that he would not let them see the land that the LORD had sworn to their fathers to give to us, a land flowing with milk and honey. 7 So it was their children, whom he raised up in their place, that Joshua circumcised. For they were uncircumcised, because they had not been circumcised on the way. Joshua 5:6-7 These verses remind us that even though they were circumcised before they left Egypt, their hearts were not changed. Some people are baptized and yet they show no change in their behavior. They don't trust God any more than they did before their baptism. This reminds us that outward signs are not what makes the change but are merely our declaration that we *claim* to be changed. It is possible to go through a ritual without experiencing what the ritual represents.

Again, we have an emphasis on obeying the voice of God. Their fathers did not enter the land because they refused to obey His voice (Hebrews 4:6). After all the miracles He did for them to set them free and bring them to the land, they still would not believe. God was giving them a land fit for herds and crops (milk and honey), but they refused to trust Him and accept it out of fear for their personal safety. God had delivered them from the Egyptian army and armies on the way to Canaan, but they feared He couldn't defeat the giants in the land. They were looking to their own ability and ignoring God.

The promises of God cannot fail (Joshua 21:45)! If they would not obey, God would raise up a generation that would. That generation consisted of those whom Joshua circumcised at Gilgal. They would receive the promises given to Abraham. They received them by faith. The enemy was still behind their walled cities. No battles had been fought, but they were willing to act in faith in the 400-year-old promise because they knew God cannot lie (Numbers 23:19).

God had encouraged their faith with some amazing miracles like drying up the Jordan River at flood stage, and hasn't God shown Himself faithful to us? We can look back to the cross and know how faithful He was to redeem us. And we can also look at things in our lives and recognize the hand of God guiding us to faith and encouraging us with things that had to be much more than coincidences. Will we take hold of the promises of God and step out in faith because we know God cannot lie? Or will we choose to remain in the wilderness and die there? What has God been placing on your heart? Will you trust Him to bring it to pass in your life by stepping out in faith?

8 When the circumcising of the whole nation was finished, they remained in their places in the camp until they were healed. Joshua 5:8 So they took a pause until they healed. The Jerichoans must have wondered what in the world was going on that the encampment of Israel grew so quiet for so long. But the fear of God kept the army of Jericho from attacking (Joshua 2:10,11). God honored Israel's obedience. And God will honor our obedience. The things we fear are in God's hands. If He should let them come to pass, they will end up being for our good.

There is a two-fold use of a Hebrew word in verses 6 and 8. It is the word translated perished in verse 6 and finished in verse 8. The author was contrasting the difference in the two armies. Both were circumcised, but one *died* in the wilderness and the other inherited the land. Both were outwardly religious, but the younger generation had a heart of faith. *Thus the earlier generation 'finished' in the death of disobedience, while the generation of Gilgal 'finished' the act of obedience.*[vii] Every one of us will finish in one of those two ways!

⁹ *And the LORD said to Joshua, "Today I have rolled away the reproach of Egypt from you." And so the name of that place is called Gilgal to this day.* Joshua 5:9 Gilgal sounds like the Hebrew word for roll. This act of faith rolled away the reproach of Egypt from them. There are various ideas for what this means, but my guess is that it means the influence of Egypt's ways and gods had affected their fathers, but this act of faith broke that cycle. The obedience to the covenant even when it left them vulnerable showed their total trust in God's power and faithfulness. This was the final severing of Egypt from the hearts of Israel. Having gone through baptism of the Jordan crossing, they were now in the new land with a new chapter of Israel's history. The next chapter would for the most part be one of faith and obedience. It reminds us of Romans 12:1,2. They were presenting their bodies as living sacrifices, holy and acceptable to God, which was their spiritual act of worship.

What a glorious blessing it is to know that God rolled away the reproach of the world from our lives when we accepted the fact that our sins were upon Jesus as He suffered and died as a just punishment for those sins! Our shame is taken away. The enemy of our soul often points to our sinful past and tries to condemn us (Revelation 12:10). We only need to point to the cross and declare that our debt was paid in full. No more guilt for our past or shame in who we once were. And even now when our thoughts do not honor God, we confess our failure and see God's justice was satisfied on the cross for those sins too. We are clean from the world's garbage (1 John 1:9). That is what Jesus was illustrating when He washed the disciples' feet. It was a picture of what He was about to do (John 13:7,8). To be in Christ is to have no more shame. We are more than debt free, we are credited with the righteousness of God in Jesus, spotless! That is what makes us ready to go in and claim the spiritual land that God has for us. He prepared good works in advance for us to step into (Ephesians 2:10). His victorious life in us will flow out from us when we step out in obedient faith.

¹⁰ While the people of Israel were encamped at Gilgal, they kept the Passover on the fourteenth day of the month in the evening on the plains of Jericho. Joshua 5:10 How fitting that before they engage in the conquest of Canaan, they renewed the covenant God made with Abraham and celebrated the deliverance in Egypt that came with the Passover. It reminded them that the God who brought them out of bondage had now brought them into the Promised Land. God brings us out of this world's bondage to sin to bring us into the promised land of life and freedom in Christ. The Holy Spirit is a deposit of that life, guaranteeing we will experience the fulness of it when we enter the promised land of heaven (Ephesians 1:13,14).

Passover was instituted when the angel of death passed over the Jewish homes in Egypt because of the blood of the lambs on the doorposts of their homes. It wasn't because the children of Israel were righteous. They deserved to die like the firstborn of Egypt died. They were just as sinful, but God provided a substitute. The Passover lamb was slain and eaten by the family in each household. The blood on the doorposts was the blood of a lamb. It pointed forward to the lamb of God who would die for our sins so that the angel of the second death would pass over us (John 1:29).

We will see in the next passage that God doesn't pick people because of how good they are. He calls those who will receive conviction and place their faith in *His* ability to make them righteous. He doesn't choose those who try the hardest, for they think they can be good enough without Him. That is the sin of pride. He calls those who know they need Him, those who will humble themselves and trust in Him alone (1 Corinthians 1:26-29).

[11] And the day after the Passover, on that very day, they ate of the produce of the land, unleavened cakes and parched grain. [12] And the manna ceased the day after they ate of the produce of the land. And there was no longer manna for the people of Israel, but they ate of the fruit of the land of Canaan that year. Joshua 5:11-12 They were probably taking the grain from the fields of Jericho to make their unleavened cakes and parched grain. The food was unleavened because they were celebrating Passover for a week (the feast of unleavened bread - Leviticus 23:6). The next morning out of habit they would have risen to collect their manna for the day, but there was none. Manna was provision for the wilderness, but now they are home in the land flowing with milk and honey.

It reminds me of our daily devotional readings. We have someone's writing on a passage that helps us apply the Scripture and understand it better. We will need it all through this life. But when we arrive in our heavenly home, we will not need a person to explain it. The Lord Himself, the living Word, will illuminate the Scriptures in ways that are beyond our present comprehension. Maybe that is what the Scripture means when it says the Lord will be our everlasting light (Isaiah 60:19). When we eat of that heavenly produce of that land, we will know our wandering in the wilderness is over.

We often speak of our life as a journey. We are looking for home, a place of rest, a place where we feel we truly belong. Does your journey feel like wilderness wandering? Are you tired of your daily routine and wandering if there is more on the other side of the Jordan? What we are reading about tells us there is! The lives of saints that have gone before us declare there is. But Gilgal is where it begins. The circumcision of the heart is the first step. It is an end of trusting in self and a surrender to all that God has for you.

I am not declaring it is easier, but I am telling you it is a lot more fulfilling. You can do everything to the glory of God (1 Corinthians 10:31), and that gives our actions meaning. Jesus promises to never leave us or forsake us (Matthew 28:20). He promises to work everything we go through for our good (Romans 8:28). He even tells us He will transform us into the likeness of Jesus (Romans 8:29). The promised land of the kingdom of God lies before us. Will you let your shame be rolled away by the circumcision of your heart? Will you join that Passover feast knowing the blood of the Lamb of God has delivered you from the second death (1 Corinthians 5:7)? Then you are ready to enter the kingdom and take the land for our King.

Questions:
1 Why can we make spiritual applications from what took place?
2 What united them as a people?
3 Why did it take faith to obey God's command?
4 What story did they know that would concern them?
5 How does circumcision foreshadow baptism?
6 What are our enemies today?
7 How was our reproach rolled away?
8 In what ways does Passover convey the same message?
9 Why did the manna cease?
10 What land are we taking?

The Commander Joshua 5:13-6:7

The nation of Israel had entered the Promised Land when God miraculously dried up the Jordan River at flood stage. Then God asked them to take a great step of faith by circumcising all the men leaving them vulnerable before their enemies. That was necessary for them to celebrate the Passover, just as it is necessary for us to be born-again pictured in baptism for us to celebrate Christ our Passover in communion (1 Corinthians 5:7). The nation had consecrated themselves to live according to God's instructions. They were ready to begin the conquest of the land, but they needed God's directions. God had promised to drive out the enemies. How would He do that?

Joshua must have gone out of the camp at Gilgal, perhaps to pray and seek God's guidance. I wonder if he was looking for vulnerabilities in the walls of Jericho. Had he learned the lesson that it is God who gives the victory? When are we expected to try to figure things out and make plans while hoping for inspiration, and when are we to wait until God gives miraculous direction? I think all believers struggle with this. Do we go with what we already have been shown, or do we wait for specific instructions? It seems to me life is mixed with these two ways. We rarely know just what God is doing, but we should always be obeying the truth we know while we wait for His specific guidance. That is the life of faith.

What lay before Joshua was definitely one of those times when he needed divine intervention. Before the conquest of the land began, Joshua needed the reassurance that he was under the authority of the God of Abraham. The Lord had parted the Jordan River, but now they were facing forces that caused their fathers to retreat in fear (Numbers 13:32). Once their fathers heard of the consequences of their lack of faith in God, they decided to go ahead and attack, but God was not with them and they were defeated (Numbers 14:44,45). Now Joshua is facing those armies. He needed to be reassured that God was with Him and would direct him. What was God's plan for the battle?

[13] When Joshua was by Jericho, he lifted up his eyes and looked, and behold, a man was standing before him with his drawn sword in his hand. And Joshua went to him and said to him, "Are you for us, or for our adversaries?" [14] And he said, "No; but I am the commander of the army of the LORD. Now I have come." And Joshua fell on his face to the earth and worshiped and said to him, "What does my lord say to his servant?" Joshua 5:13-14 Joshua must have had his head bowed in prayer, for when he looked up, he suddenly saw he was face to face with a man with a drawn sword. He asked whose side the man was on. That is the natural question to ask. Perhaps it was someone from another tribe wanting to be an ally. Two verses later the warrior will be called YHWH, the eternal covenant God of Israel.[viii] Joshua had to sense this "man" was a supernatural being. The answer is very strange. "No!" Some translations take the little negative Hebrew word to mean "neither". That is fascinating. Once we realize He is the pre-incarnate Christ, why wouldn't He say, "I'm on your side"? That is because He is for everyone. He is not willing that any should eternally perish (2 Peter 3:9). All of Jericho, except for Rahab and her family, are on the other side. God does not take sides. He is on His own side, the side of righteousness, truth, justice, but also mercy and love.

The being declared, *"I am the commander of the army of the Lord."* That is the same as saying that He is YHWH Saba, the LORD of hosts, the God of angel armies, which is one of God's names (1 Samuel 1:3). That is why Joshua responded by falling on his face and worshiping Him. Some people refer to this as a Theophany and others as a Christophany. Jesus is the visible manifestation of the invisible God (Colossians 1:15) and so I prefer to call it a Christophany, an appearance of Jesus before the incarnation. Angels will not allow men to bow before them in submission, for that is a form of worship (Revelation 22:9). It is unthinkable that an angel of God would allow himself to be referred to as YHWH! This is one of the clearest appearances of Jesus in the Old Testament. Yehoshua/Joshua is standing before the God/man he is foreshadowing whose name in Aramaic will be the same as his, Yeshua.

A later prophet named Elisha was surrounded by the Syrian army. His servant was so frightened that Elisha prayed that the eyes of his servant would be opened to see that there were more with them than there were with their enemies. He could see the hills surrounding them covered with chariots of fire (2 Kings 6:17). That is the army this Commander leads. And if these are His forces, what earthly enemy can stand against Him? Joshua was being reminded that it is not up to his army to take Jericho, but the Lord of heaven and earth. The battle belongs to the Lord (Proverbs 21:31).

If Joshua had any remaining doubts after seeing the Jordan dry and hearing of the fear the inhabitants of the land had, now he should be completely assured that God is with him as He was with Moses. He is meeting face to face with Him as Moses did (Exodus 33:11), for Jesus would later say that if you have seen me you have seen the Father (John 14:9).

Joshua was facing a task that seemed impossible but knowing that God was directing him would make all the difference. I don't know what you are facing: illness, uncertainty about tomorrow, doubts, fears, betrayals, heartache, or temptations, and what we all face, the world, our flesh, and the devil. We need the same reassurance that Joshua needed. Are we with the Commander of the Lord's armies? Are we letting Him lead?

Joshua shows his heart in his response to Jesus' declaration about Himself. *"What does my lord say to his servant?"* In other words, "I am waiting for your command." That should always be our question when we sense the Lord is present, when our heart is made aware that it is time for Him to speak to us. When we face the insurmountable issue that lies before us, this should be our question. It is what the high priest Eli told little Samuel to respond to the Lord when he heard his name called: *"Speak Lord, your servant is listening"* (1 Samuel 3:9). We acknowledge His lordship over our lives and our place as His servants and our duty to hear and obey. We look to His Word and see what He has already commanded us. We go to prayer and ask Him to impress on our hearts the specifics of how we should go about obeying.

15 And the commander of the LORD's army said to Joshua, "Take off your sandals from your feet, for the place where you are standing is holy." And Joshua did so. Joshua 5:15 Joshua probably heard Moses' account of the burning bush a hundred times (Exodus 3:5). Now the very words God spoke to Moses are spoken to him.

Jesus' presence makes any ordinary place holy! That is why the Bible calls us saints. His presence is in us (John 14:23). Sometimes when we worship together, I become so aware of His presence that I take off my shoes and drop to my knees. It happens in times of prayer as well. He is always with us, for He has promised to never leave us or forsake us, but there are times when our focus shifts from the physical world around us and we are overwhelmed by the sense of His glorious presence. We need those moments like Joshua needed this encounter. But we can't stay there, or we would be of little earthly good. Those moments prepare us for the battles we face.

The presence of the Lord is overwhelming love, but it is also instructional. Like Joshua, we look at our problems that seem like a dark shroud over us, and suddenly the light bursts through. In prayer or the reading of God's Word, the answer suddenly becomes clear. God has spoken and given us His direction. We no longer ask if He is on our side. We declare that we are on His side. It is a matter of who is in charge. This truth gives us a whole new perspective on the problems we face. They are no longer our problems but His. The burden comes off our shoulders, and we realize all we must do is follow His lead.

The commander of the army of the LORD told Joshua the same thing the voice from the burning bush told Moses. The ground is holy because the Most Holy is standing on it, and what He touches becomes holy. God asked Moses and Joshua to take of their sandals for the same reason Jesus washed the feet of the disciples' feet (John 13). Our feet are what constantly come in contact with this world. The dirt that clings to our shoes represents the contamination of this fallen world. Putting our shoes aside represents us putting aside worldly distractions and uncleanness. Where Jesus manifests His presence is holy and holiness will not abide that which is unholy (Habakkuk 1:13a).

Jewish commentators have long recognized that a being appears periodically in the Old Testament who completely represents God. They refer to Him as the Prince of the Countenances.[ix] In other words, the faces of God. Well, think for a moment what the title means. A prince is the son of the king. There you have it. Jesus is the Son of God and perfectly represents the Father, so Jesus could say, *"I and my Father are one"* (John 10:30).

Here is the path to victory over the conflicts we face. We don't need to develop good plans. We need to be obedient to our Commander. That only comes when we fall on our faces before Him in full submission and reverence to do His will, hear His voice, and get up and obey. When we realize the battle is not ours but the LORD's, then we can go forward in obedience with assurance that the outcome belongs to the LORD (2 Chronicles 20:15).

¹ Now Jericho was shut up inside and outside because of the people of Israel. None went out, and none came in. Joshua 6:1 Shut up inside and outside reminds me of the stay in home orders during the Corona virus. Since the fear of the God of Israel had come upon Jericho, they did not venture out to battle. Nor would they let anyone go out lest they be captured and made to give information about the city. The leaders of Jericho were hoping the Israelites could not penetrate their walls.

² And the LORD said to Joshua, "See, I have given Jericho into your hand, with its king and mighty men of valor. Joshua 6:2 The angel is speaking but the text says YHWH said to Joshua… The LORD told Joshua He had given Jericho, its king, and its soldiers into the hand of Joshua. That is past tense. It is already done. We need to realize the promises of God are as good as done, for God is outside of time and sees them already fulfilled (2 Corinthians 1:20). When God tells us something, there is no reason to ever doubt it. We may not understand the process or timing, but we can be sure it will come to pass. This declaration to Joshua is like a rock on which he can stand. The rest of the instructions tell how he is to go about seeing it come to pass.

In a larger sense, God has already told him that everywhere the soles of his feet tread will be given him (Deuteronomy 11:24). This first battle in the Promised Land is a pattern, not in the details of how to take a city, but that in each case he was to look to the LORD for the tactic and trust Him to bring it to pass. God's instructions are not so much about the soldiers' actions, but that the ark of the covenant goes with them. If God is with them who can be against them (Romans 8:31)?

That pattern has never changed. The Great Commission tells us to go into all the world and make disciples of all nations, teaching them what Christ has commanded us and baptizing them. It is preceded with the declaration that all authority in heaven and on earth is given to Jesus. It is followed by the declaration that He is with us always even to the end of the age (Matthew 28:18-20). This is the same pattern. Jesus has the authority. He has sent us out to take the land (which is our full surrender and pointing souls to Jesus). He goes with us and gives us the tactics, and by that I do not mean a method, but the leading of the Holy Spirit in each situation.

Some men follow this pattern and find great success and then write a book telling you of the tactics God gave them for their battle. Then we imitate that tactic but not the pattern of first getting our instruction from the LORD and counting on His presence. Instead, we count on the tactics in the situation described in the book and expect God to show up and do the same thing. Millions of man hours have been wasted in this way. It is easier to follow what someone has written than to wait on the LORD and get His instruction. Why? Because we must give Him control and that makes us feel out of control unless we believe His promises are an accomplished fact.

³ You shall march around the city, all the men of war going around the city once. Thus shall you do for six days. ⁴ Seven priests shall bear seven trumpets of rams' horns before the ark. Joshua 6:3,4a The LORD gave them His battle plan. All Israel's warriors were to march around the city once every day for six days. The ark of the covenant was carried by the priests preceded by seven priests with shofars who would be in the middle of the army.

When the ark was out of the temple it was always covered so that people could not look on it (Numbers 4:5).

It was surely covered when they went through the Jordan. If Jericho had spies, they would have wondered about the god who stayed covered and could do such wonders. They would see this mysterious thing going around their city and wonder what this super weapon could do.

Joshua was being asked to perform another act of faith. Marching around the city meant they would be vulnerable to arrows and rocks hurled from the city walls. God would have to restrain the enemy if Israel marched around the city day after day.

4bOn the seventh day you shall march around the city seven times, and the priests shall blow the trumpets. 5 And when they make a long blast with the ram's horn, when you hear the sound of the trumpet, then all the people shall shout with a great shout, and the wall of the city will fall down flat, and the people shall go up, everyone straight before him." Joshua 6:4b,5 On the seventh day they were to march around the walls seven times and then blow the trumpets and give a great battle shout. Then the walls would fall flat, and they were to march straight in. It reminds me of some of the wild things God told His people to do in the past such as building a giant boat when they had never seen rain (Genesis 6:13,14), or to throw a stick in the water to make and axe head float (2 Kings 6:6). What kind of assault is this seven-day march? And why seven times on the seventh day? Isn't that going to wear out the soldiers? Wouldn't it be better to take lessons on how to scale walls? Or perhaps they would be better off building battering rams?

God's ways are higher than man's ways, as the heavens are higher than the earth (Isaiah 55:8,9). He does the unexpected that is often contrary to what man would think so that He gets the glory. I think God delights in showing us that He is the One in charge and is watching over us and working through us despite our weaknesses.

He delights in using the least likely, the simple and the weak (1 Corinthians 1:26-29).

⁶ So Joshua the son of Nun called the priests and said to them, "Take up the ark of the covenant and let seven priests bear seven trumpets of rams' horns before the ark of the LORD." ⁷ And he said to the people, "Go forward. March around the city and let the armed men pass on before the ark of the LORD." Joshua 6:6,7 So Joshua did exactly what Jesus told him to do. Did he tell anyone the plan? What did they think after each day's march? If it were not for the miraculous crossing of the Jordan, there might have been some rebellion over this seemingly ineffective plan. But it seems they all had faith that Joshua heard from the LORD to the same degree that Moses did.

We should certainly have faith that our Joshua, the Lord Jesus, spoke the words His Father gave Him. He is still the Commander of angel armies. In addition, He has given us spiritual weapons to fight alongside the heavenly army. They are not carnal weapons, but they are weapons mighty through God. They pull down arguments and everything that exalts itself against God. We take every thought captive and make it obedient to Christ (2 Corinthians 10:4,5). He has given us great authority to pray His will into the earth. When our prayers come from a heart surrendered to God's will, they cause the enemy to tremble. And with this army and these weapons and the presence of our invincible Commander, we cannot lose. What seems to be losses are only steps to greater victories.

And yet we look at low church attendance, loved ones addicted to drugs or alcohol, the decline in our own culture, the divorce rate and prevalence of abortion and we wonder what we can do. We make our plans, read of others' successes, have our prayer meetings and conferences. We do our best only to find we are losing ground. That is when we wonder away from the camp and look to the heavens and suddenly come face to face with the Commander.

It was right to challenge the unknown warrior, for John tells us to test the spirits (1 John 4:1). But Joshua's mistake was to assume this One was on his side or the enemy's side. We must always realize that there is only God's side versus all that is opposed to His goodness. Then He gives us a plan that we would never have thought of.

As we continue our journey through Joshua, we will be reminded that our Commander single handedly won the final battle on the cross (Colossians 2:13-15). Who of us would have come up with God's plan to restore mankind to Himself through the cross? That is one reason we can know man didn't make up this gospel (Galatians 1:11).

To get an idea of how great a warrior our Commander is, remember that He let men do their worst, allowed Satan and his demons to fight Him with His hands and feet nailed in place, and He still won. He walked out of the grave with the keys of death and hell. He is the greatest of all warriors. And if we want to learn to fight this spiritual battle, we look to how He fought it with the Word of God as His weapon. He didn't do anything on His own. He looked to see what the Father was doing. (John 5:19). Learn from the best! Listen to the Commander of heaven's armies, and do what He says (Luke 1:38; James 1:22).

Questions:
1 What was Joshua's question and the angel's answer?
2 Who does the angel declare Himself to be?
3 What is His first command to Joshua? Why?
4 What does this mean to Joshua?
5 Why does God say the battle is won?
6 What is the battle plan?
7 Would it be the same for future battles? Lesson?

8 What is our overall battle plan?
9 What are our weapons?
10 How do we fight our battles?

Separated Joshua 6:8-27

Last week we read the account of Joshua receiving the instructions for the conquest of Jericho from the Commander of the hosts of heaven. It was a strange plan that sounded impractical. Joshua certainly needed faith to obey, but after that supernatural encounter, his faith was surely bolstered. Joshua relayed the strange commands to the people, and in our passage today they set out following his orders that came from the ultimate Commander.

8 And just as Joshua had commanded the people, the seven priests bearing the seven trumpets of rams' horns before the LORD went forward, blowing the trumpets, with the ark of the covenant of the LORD following them. 9 The armed men were walking before the priests who were blowing the trumpets, and the rear guard was walking after the ark, while the trumpets blew continually. Joshua 6:8,9 We get a few more details about how the procession was formed in these verses. The army went first, then the seven priests with the shofars, and then the ark of the covenant, followed by a rear guard. The Lord, represented by the ark, is in the middle. The trumpets blew the entire time they circled the city.

I want us to pay attention to a point barely mentioned but that we see throughout Scripture. The ark of the covenant represents the Lord in the middle of the procession. When we look at how they were to camp as they went through the wilderness, the tabernacle was in the center of the camp. In the Garden of Eden, the tree of Life was in the midst of the Garden (Genesis 2:9). Jesus promised if two or more are gathered in His name that He

82

is in their midst (Matthew 18:20). The closest one can be to every person is in the center of the group. I think the language is telling us that God wants to be as close as possible to every one of His people (Zephaniah 3:17). Were there individual soldiers who requested to be on the back of the column that went before the ark or did some in the rear guard ask to be at the front so they could be close to the ark? Were there those in the wilderness camp who asked to be able to put their tents as far as possible from the tribe of Levi that surrounded the tabernacle?

God tells us that if we draw near to Him that He will draw near to us (James 4:8a). But there is a respectful fear of Him. He is after all, a consuming fire (Deuteronomy 4:24). He purifies and refines (Deuteronomy 23:14; Isaiah 4:4). Surely there were those who wanted to be as far as possible from Him. Others may have been comfortable in the middle somewhere. But some souls wanted the refinement, the purifying, that comes from drawing near (Hebrews 10:22). Where do you want to be?

10 But Joshua commanded the people, "You shall not shout or make your voice heard, neither shall any word go out of your mouth, until the day I tell you to shout. Then you shall shout." 11 So he caused the ark of the LORD to circle the city, going about it once. And they came into the camp and spent the night in the camp. Joshua 6:10,11 There was one more command. They were not to say a word as they marched. No songs! No chit chat! Not a noise was to be heard from their mouths until Joshua told them to shout. It represented the solemnity of impending judgment.

I can imagine the conversations around the campfire that night. "Why aren't we building a battering ram and ladders?" "Are we going to do this tomorrow too?" "What in the world is Joshua up to?" "What does he think will happen when we shout?"

12 Then Joshua rose early in the morning, and the priests took up the ark of the LORD. 13 And the seven priests bearing the seven trumpets of rams' horns before the ark of the LORD walked on, and they blew the trumpets continually. And the armed men were walking before them, and the rear guard was walking after the ark of the LORD, while the trumpets blew continually. 14 And the second day they marched around the city once, and returned into the camp. So they did for six days. Joshua 6:12-14 Day after day for six days it was the same routine. First thing in the morning they persistently obeyed the command. That required patient trust that Joshua had heard from God. It took faith that the God of their fathers was protecting them and had a plan they didn't understand.

What would you have said? What do you say when you obey the Lord and nothing seems to be different? He says you are a new creation (2 Corinthians 5:17), but you keep doing battle with the flesh. He says He will finish the work He started in you (Philippians 1:6), but at the rate you are going, you think you would have to live as long as Methuselah. Study your Bible, pray, fellowship, day after day after day. When do we get to shout? When will the walls fall down? The Lord says the victory is ours for He has conquered, but we are still in the battle. Do you see the parallel? But the final day is coming. If we will trust, obey, and patiently persevere, we to will see the promises of God come to pass. God cannot fail. The work He started in you will be completed.

15 On the seventh day they rose early, at the dawn of day, and marched around the city in the same manner seven times. It was only on that day that they marched around the city seven times. 16 And at the seventh time, when the priests had blown the trumpets, Joshua said to the people, "Shout, for the LORD has given you the city. [17] And the city and all that is within it shall be devoted to the LORD for destruction. Only Rahab the prostitute and all who are with her in her house shall live, because she hid the messengers whom we sent. Joshua 6:15-17 Finally, at the end of the seven rounds on the seventh day... but first more instruction. The city is to be utterly destroyed. Only the useful metals are to be retrieved for the future temple. This is because the wickedness of the people has reached such a state over the last 400 years that God commanded that nothing in Jericho remain (Genesis 15:16). The metals can be purified by fire. What harmful viruses and bacteria were in the clothing and other things in the city? They represent the sin that permeated the culture. The entire city was hardened beyond repentance except for the family of Rahab. It was therefore to be destroyed.

Only Rahab and her family were to be saved. This means they were considered sanctified by faith (Acts 26:18; Ephesians 2:8,9). That is the only way to escape the wrath of God. She already acknowledged that the LORD was God in heaven and in earth (Joshua 2:11). This is one of the many examples that God was not just randomly picking the Jewish nation alone but working through the nation to draw people from every culture to Himself (Acts 10:34,35).

[18] But you, keep yourselves from the things devoted to destruction, lest when you have devoted them you take any of the devoted things and make the camp of Israel a thing for destruction and bring trouble upon it. [19] But all silver and gold, and every vessel of bronze and iron, are holy to the LORD; they shall go into the treasury of the LORD." Joshua 6:18,19 I encourage you to mark these two verses. This is a major theme in the Law/Torah and the New Testament. There are two kinds of salvation. There is salvation of the soul, when we look to Jesus to forgive us

and accept the forgiveness merited when He took our punishment upon Himself on the cross. The Israelites looked forward to this in their daily sacrifices and especially on the Day of Atonement.

The other kind of salvation is a result of being a child of God who yields to the lordship of Jesus. Paul calls it salvation from this present evil age (Galatians 1:4). It is pictured in the Israelites deliverance and separation from Egypt.

The Laws of Moses have many instructions for not mixing things, a picture of not being entwined in this fallen world. Here in this passage, we see it in the instructions to totally destroy Jericho. Moses had told them that was the way they were to conquer the land so that the pagan influences did not draw them from the Lord (Deuteronomy 7:1-5). Only that which could be sanctified by fire was to be kept for the treasury of the LORD (Numbers 31:23).

In the New Testament we are told that in the end our works will be tested by fire as well. The wood, hay, and stubble will burn up. Only the precious metal will remain and are dedicated to the Lord (1 Corinthians 3:12,13). It is describing the meaningless works of the flesh that have nothing to do with spiritual life. It is like building a house in Sodom or Jericho. It will pass away with those cities. That which remains is that which belongs to God. Do you belong to God? Do your actions come from His life in you? Do you live to glorify Him? That is precious, golden, and not of this passing world. (2 Corinthians 6:17; Revelation 18:4 from Isaiah 52:11).

We used to say, "Only one life, will soon be past, only what's done for Christ will last." I change that to say, "only what is done *by* Christ will last." We do a lot of things for the Lord that are not at His instruction and without His power - wood, hay, and stubble. But when He leads us and we look to His inspiration and power, then there is fruit that remains. In other words, it is golden, for it is for the glory of God.

Sin, which is disobedience to our good God, caused us to be ejected from a perfect world and into a cursed one. We gave up our authority over the world to Satan, and that is why he is called the ruler of this world (John 12:31). Nature is not evil, but it is under a curse. Our old desires and Satan's temptation is to worship the world and the things in the world (1 John 2:15-17). We want the gold for ourselves, in other words for our glory and not God's. That is the problem we will see in the next chapter. But then it is not sanctified. Sanctified means for God's use alone. And by our taking the cursed things for our use alone, we then bring that curse upon ourselves.

Set your hearts on things above and not on things of the earth (Colossians 3:1,2). Lay up your treasures in heaven, not on the earth where moth and rust corrupt it (Matthew 6:19,20). Do not conform to the world but be transformed by the renewing of your minds (Romans 12:2). I could go on and on with verses that tell us to be saved from this present evil world. It is walking in the Spirit and not in the flesh, which is the old fallen nature that included your passions before you came to Christ. We live in Christ or we live in the world. We can't straddle the two. If we are in Christ, we serve Him continually and enjoy the good gifts of God and give Him thanks for them. In the world we try to satisfy our emptiness with the things of the world and always think we need just a little more. God ordains us to be stewards over some of this world's things so we can use them for His glory. But we can only do that when we put Him first.

[20] So the people shouted, and the trumpets were blown. As soon as the people heard the sound of the trumpet, the people shouted a great shout, and the wall fell down flat, so that the people went up into the city, every

man straight before him, and they captured the city.
²¹ Then they devoted all in the city to destruction, both men and women, young and old, oxen, sheep, and donkeys, with the edge of the sword. Joshua 6:20,21 The army was to let out a shout along with the long trumpet blasts (Isaiah 58:1). When they did, the walls fell down flat. That they collapsed all at once is a miracle. That it did not end up as a pile to climb over was another miracle. They charged in and took the city. Now that is shock and awe! Every animal and everyone who was not killed in the collapse of the walls were killed.

That is shocking to us today, but I want you to remember that it was God's judgment not man's. God put up with their increased wickedness, their slaughter of babies, the sexual worship of demons, the centuries of provoking God, until the degree of wickedness was like that of the world before the great flood (Genesis 15:16; Deuteronomy 9:5). If any survived who did not honor the God of Israel, they would soon be leading people to their seductive idolatry (Leviticus 18:24,25). And in fact, that is what would happen in the future because Israel did not remove all the people from the land. The compromise ended in the captivity of the people of Israel. God knew the condition of every heart, their potential future, and what they would become had they survived. God is always just in all His decrees because He knows every detail. Judgment only comes when all else has failed to turn a people from their descent into depravity.

The only way this could happen in our day is by natural calamities or what insurance companies rightly call "acts of God." Do good people perish with the wicked? Yes, and we see that several times in the Bible. The wicked often kill the messengers who are warning them. But for us, death is only a graduation into glory. When ISIS would destroy a Christian village because it refused to convert,

God knew. He welcomes the martyrs home and wipes the tears from their eyes (Revelation 7:17). God rarely directly intervenes in judgment like this, but it does happen in our day as well.

I read an account of an ISIS group that was planning an attack on a city. They were in a pit on a hill overlooking the city and making their evil plans when a herd of wild boars attacked and killed them. To Muslims, that is the worst possible way to die as they see pigs as unclean animals. I have also read of firsthand accounts of Jesus appearing to members of ISIS leading to their conversion. Those individuals were like Rahab in Jericho. God knows the hearts that are truly seeking Him.

22 But to the two men who had spied out the land, Joshua said, "Go into the prostitute's house and bring out from there the woman and all who belong to her, as you swore to her." 23 So the young men who had been spies went in and brought out Rahab and her father and mother and brothers and all who belonged to her. And they brought all her relatives and put them outside the camp of Israel. Joshua 6:22,23 Joshua sent the two spies who had made the pact with Rahab to bring her and her family out. It would be easy to see where they were, as it was the only part of the wall left standing, which was another miracle. Faith rescued them from the judgement of God on the city.

I want to emphasize this point because people often ask about the innocent people who never heard of Jesus. Rahab only knew of what the God of Israel had done for Israel. She heard testimonies as news and her heart began to wonder about a God who could do those things. Then she committed herself to Him and even risking her life to hide the spies. God used the news that traders brought to touch her heart. Why didn't it touch the hearts of others in the city? It is the same reason people hear of what Jesus has done for us and how He conquered the grave and yet refuse the drawing of the Holy Spirit. Mankind does not want to give up his ways, pride, or independence.

They put Rahab and her family outside the camp. Before we are welcomed into the family of God, we need to put away all the impurity, renounce the old gods we worshiped, and understand what it is we are becoming a part of. We often try to bring in our old ideas that we had before and try to blend them with the revelation of Scripture. There may be a nugget of truth in what we once believed, but we must allow the Word of God to interpret what is true and separate it from what is not.

24 And they burned the city with fire, and everything in it. Only the silver and gold, and the vessels of bronze and of iron, they put into the treasury of the house of the LORD. 25 But Rahab the prostitute and her father's household and all who belonged to her, Joshua saved alive. And she has lived in Israel to this day, because she hid the messengers whom Joshua sent to spy out Jericho. 26 Joshua laid an oath on them at that time, saying, "Cursed before the LORD be the man who rises up and rebuilds this city, Jericho. "At the cost of his firstborn shall he lay its foundation, and at the cost of his youngest son shall he set up its gates." 27 So the LORD was with Joshua, and his fame was in all the land. Joshua 6:24-27 Everything that could burn was burned. Only Rahab and her family were spared because of her faith in the God of Israel demonstrated in hiding the spies. Rahab is welcomed into the nation as Gentile convert. She even becomes one of the ancestors of David and of our Messiah, Jesus (Matthew 1:5)! This emphasizes God's heart to bring into the family of God all who will come to Him in faith, regardless of their past. They are the true descendants of Abraham, the father of the people of faith (Romans 4:16).

There is a town called Jericho today. It is not the city Joshua conquered, for that city is still a massive pile of rock and bricks. It was rebuilt and Joshua's curse came to pass (1 Kings 16:34). If the people of Canaan feared the Israelites because of what they heard about them leaving Egypt and events in the wilderness, now they would be trembling as the news of the annihilation of the walled city of Jericho reached them. God was preparing the way for the conquest of the entire land He had promised to Abraham's descendants.

In our day, the Commander has given us quite a different set of instructions. Our struggle is not against flesh and blood, but against evil in the heavenly realms, in our hearts, and the hearts of others (2 Corinthians 10:3-5). Our weapons are not physical things but love, prayer, and faithful obedience to our Commander's instructions. We are not taking a piece of land and setting up an earthly kingdom, for our citizenship is in heaven (Philippians 3:20). We are to love our enemies and pray for those who persecute us. Ephesians 6 tells us our defense is faith, the helmet of salvation, the belt of truth, the breastplate of righteousness, and our offensive weapon is the Word of God. Our feet are always to be fitted with the gospel of peace.

In the spiritual realm we tear down strongholds and take every thought captive and make it obedient to Christ. We devote our bodies as living sacrifices, holy and acceptable to God because of Jesus' sacrifice for us. Our Commander is leading us to take a spiritual promised land where we desire the sincere milk of the Word and find it sweeter than honey (Psalm 19:10; 1 Peter 2:2). Christ our King goes before us and our shouts of praise bring down walls opposition and set the captives free (Matthew 16:18). Are you engaged in the battle, suited up, and ready for the Commander's instructions?

Questions:

1 How did Joshua get this command?
2 Why did the people obey what sounded crazy?
3 What were the details of the plan?
4 What is significant about the ark in the middle of the army?
5 What would you have thought after three or four days?
6 How does that relate to our routines and obedience?
7 What was an additional miracle in the way the walls fell?
8 Why did everything need to be destroyed? Analogy?
9 How were Rahab and family saved?
10 How do we do battle today?

Defeated! Joshua 7:1-9

Previously we read of the conquest of Jericho and God's strict instructions to destroy everything except the metals. Those metals were to be cleansed by fire and dedicated to God and were eventually used for the future temple. The utter destruction of everything in Jericho was God's judgment on the spiritual condition of the city. It was an indication of how separate God's people are to be from the depravity of the world. As Jesus indicated, we are to be in the world but not of the world (John 17:16).

I will remind you often that the theocratic nation of Israel was one-time event in world history. God directed them to carry out His will. No nations since have been so clearly directed by God. God does use nations to judge other nations (1 Chronicles 5:26), but we see in Scripture that God holds them accountable when they are excessively cruel (Jeremiah 25:12). The judgment on the people of Canaan came after 400 years of increasingly depraved behavior and worship of demonic gods.

The land had become defiled by the activities of the people of the land. If Israel took their possessions, they too would become defiled (6:18). God does not have a double standard. This was not about ethnicity. Depravity is just as evil if not more so when it is exhibited by the people of God. This cleansing by fire was a physical picture of a spiritual reality. It is true in a spiritual sense for God's people today.

There are numerous things that defile our culture: pornography, political deception and hatred, bribery, injustice, the destruction of genders, hedonism, and perhaps most prevalent of all, the worship of wealth. Every born-again follower of Jesus should destroy these things from their life. We cannot tolerate them, or we will cease to be a follower of Jesus. What fellowship does light have with darkness (2 Corinthians 6:14)? If we are clinging to worldliness, we eventually become an enemy of God (James 4:4).

The history of Israel bares out this theme. They would draw close to God and obey His commands and prosper. In their prosperity they would stop looking to God and increasingly desire the things the pagans had. The culture would then decline and eventually be overcome by their enemies. Then they would cry out to God and the cycle would begin again. It is obvious where our nation is in the cycle. More importantly, where are you in the cycle? May God help us to always passionately and purposefully dedicate ourselves to love and obey our Savior and Lord.

[1]But the people of Israel broke faith in regard to the devoted things, for Achan the son of Carmi, son of Zabdi, son of Zerah, of the tribe of Judah, took some of the devoted things. And the anger of the Lord burned against the people of Israel. Joshua 7:1 Do a search in the Scriptures for the phrase "but God." You will find God often intervening to save people from the wrath of other men. Now notice how this chapter begins, "But the people." Everything was looking great. They recommitted

themselves to God and watched God bring a miraculous victory, "but the people..."

I can say that God spared my life a number of times, *but then I* was disobedient and consequences came. Thank God He remembers our frame that we are but dust (Psalm 103:14). But when our actions turn the course of too many people in the wrong direction, God may insist on the justice we deserve. He holds us who know better to the strictest standard (James 3:1).

"Broke faith" is the term for adultery (Numbers 5:12,13). Israel had betrayed their covenant with God. This hints at the intimacy and love God had for Israel, and yet instead of responding with faithfulness, Achan responded by breaking covenant vows. One man sinned but the whole nation was charged. That doesn't seem fair. Surely no one else, except Achan's family knew what he did. So why is the nation held responsible? It is a lesson for us to examine carefully.

The conquest of Canaan was just beginning. To start off with a little disobedience would mean that before long the whole nation would be in rebellion (Acts 5:4,5). My sin does not only affect me, but it also affects my family, and my family affects my city, and my city affects my state, and my state affects the nation. We cannot sin as an island unto ourselves. We are united with others. Husband and wife are one. Those in fellowship in Christ are one. Recall Paul's body metaphor in 1 Corinthians 12. When one part of the body suffers, the rest of the body suffers with it (1 Corinthians 12:26). My disobedience affects us all. Your disobedience affects us all. If something is a little bit contaminated, it is contaminated. If I gave you a cookie and told you only a part of it had arsenic in it, you would throw away the cookie. This has a lot to do with the direction of our nation. We can whine about it, but instead, focus on influencing others toward godliness.

Americans are individualists. Most of the world is still tribal or extended family in culture. That makes it difficult for us to grasp this truth that we are not independent of others. God could not bless the nation when there was outright disobedience. Those not involved directly suffer because of what rebels against God do. We say it is not fair, but that is not because God is wrong. It is because in man's free will someone chose to rebel against God's goodness which affected others. If there is compromise in the life of an individual it affects the whole congregation.

In this chapter we will see the whole lineage of Achan back to the son of Israel listed both going backward and forward. I believe God lists it twice because we should realize that our actions also can honor or shame our ancestors. This is another cultural issue that is biblical but not acknowledged in our own culture (Exodus 20:5,6). When I lived in Japan, I could see that eastern culture was extremely aware of how their actions affected the family name. That is one reason that one of the Ten Commandments is to honor our father and mother (Exodus 20:12). A godly life honors your heritage.

2Joshua sent men from Jericho to Ai, which is near Beth-aven, east of Bethel, and said to them, "Go up and spy out the land." And the men went up and spied out Ai. 3And they returned to Joshua and said to him, "Do not have all the people go up, but let about two or three thousand men go up and attack Ai. Do not make the whole people toil up there, for they are few." Joshua 7:2,3 The people were moving north, and the first small city to the north and up in the higher country westward was Ai. The spies thought that rather than have the nation move up the mountain ridge a few thousand men should easily take it.

What was different from the siege of Jericho? What was God's plan? Who was going to fight this battle? What had begun at the direction of the Commander of the hosts of heaven was now being decided by men and their good suggestions. Their triumph had resulted in self-confidence rather than increased trust in the Lord. We all have inclinations and "good" ideas, but what does God say and who will speak for Him? Had Joshua so quickly forgotten that the battle belongs to the Lord (Proverbs 21:31)?

We, too, can rely on past spiritual victories. When all our testimonies are from years ago, we should check or present spiritual state. We are either moving onward and upward in our faith and trust in Christ, or we are slipping backward into self-confidence as if what we accomplished was done on our own. The battles before us should always be met with prayer as we wait for the Lord's direction.

⁴So about three thousand men went up there from the people. And they fled before the men of Ai, ⁵and the men of Ai killed about thirty-six of their men and chased them before the gate as far as Shebarim and struck them at the descent. And the hearts of the people melted and became as water. Joshua 7:4,5 No doubt Ai had heard of the fall of Jericho and prepared to do their best in battle. Now the sane thing for Ai to do would have been to seek a truce or flee, but God had hardened their hearts because He had enough of their wickedness. I imagine the army of Israel, seeing no resistance came to the gate and suddenly had all kinds of things dropped from above onto their soldiers followed by a massive barrage of arrows. That is just my guess, but we do know the battle quickly went south as the Israelites fled. And while fleeing down the slope into the Jordan valley, their backs were exposed and vulnerable.

The effect on Israel was disastrous as their hope and courage melted away. Now it was not the Canaanites whose hearts melted but Israel's heart (5:1). God wasn't going to collapse every wall and let them go about the conquest in their own way. This defeat came for a reason. Often defeat and grief brings us to our knees to ask God why He has allowed this pain to come into our lives. Sometimes it is to show us where we have been disobedient. God whispers to us in our good times but shouts to us through our pain. I am not implying that all pain or trouble is because we are disobedient (John 9:2,3), but that can be the case, and we should search our hearts to see if it is. There is always a reason whether we understand it or not. God is always ready to speak to us, whether for conviction or comfort. We must be eager to listen.

It is natural for us to wonder about those who died. Why them and why then? God has numbered our days (Psalm 39:4). We really can't answer that question. We know it was time for judgment on the people of Canaan, but what about these dead Jews? God knows what we would do in the future. I believe He takes us home at just the right time. It always seems too early for those who are not aged, but we must trust God that He knows best, even in the case of children. We cannot see what would have been, but God can. Only God knows what might have been.

⁶Then Joshua tore his clothes and fell to the earth on his face before the ark of the Lord until the evening, he and the elders of Israel. And they put dust on their heads. Joshua 7:6 The 72 elders and Joshua fell on their faces before the ark of the LORD. Dust on their heads was sign of grief and mourning. They were waiting to hear from the LORD, something they should have done before any plans were made. At least they knew where to turn. We might have examined the generals and tried to determine where their strategy had failed. Joshua could have placed blame on the leaders and their lack of courage to face the enemy. But Joshua learned from Moses where to turn when trouble strikes. The practical can be examined later, but first go to God and ask Him just what went wrong.

The more that we see of the might and power of God, the more we are accountable to Him. They had seen the miracles in the wilderness, the Jordan River parting, and the amazing levelling of the walls of Jericho. They should have known to seek God's direction before the attack on Ai. Who is responsible for the death of those 36 men? Joshua? Achan? The High Priest? Or is the correct answer all of Israel?

When we face defeats as a family or a congregation, we should be careful not to blame an individual, though one person may have been the source of it. The congregation should be sensitive to the Holy Spirit. Anyone and everyone should speak up. Leadership should humbly admit their failure. And all should thank God that His mercies are new every morning (Lamentations 3:22,23). I've been in a congregation that tried to hide moral failure. It permeated the whole congregation.

7And Joshua said, "Alas, O Lord God, why have you brought this people over the Jordan at all, to give us into the hands of the Amorites, to destroy us? Would that we had been content to dwell beyond the Jordan! Joshua 7:7 Joshua finally voices what is in his heart. He asks why God did not go before them? Why were they defeated? Were the Amorites going to destroy them? Wouldn't it have been better just to stay on the other side of the Jordan? We could berate Joshua for questions that were contrary to God's promises, but once again we can relate. If we had given orders that ended in losing 36 lives, husbands and fathers who would never be there for their families, we would probably pray in a similar manner. His prayer is a prayer of agony of spirit. It echoed many of the murmurings of Israel in the wilderness (Numbers 20:4; Exodus 16:3). That is what we resort to when we are despondent. We express our complaint to God when we don't understand what God has allowed. We forget about the promises of God and previous victories (1:6). But God can take it. Better to cry out to God in prayer than to keep it all inside.

⁸O Lord, what can I say, when Israel has turned their backs before their enemies! Joshua 7:8 In that type of warfare, to turn you back was to expose your vulnerable side to the enemy arrows and swords. The same is true for our spiritual warfare. The description of the armor of God in Ephesians 6 has nothing for the back. That is because we are to always be on the offensive. Greater is He who is in us than he who is in the world (1 John 4:4). We always have the superiority when it comes to spiritual battles. The Commander of the hosts is more than a match for all the forces of hell. He proved it on the cross. Don't forget that!

⁹For the Canaanites and all the inhabitants of the land will hear of it and will surround us and cut off our name from the earth. And what will you do for your great name?" Joshua 7:9 Joshua is afraid he will lose the psychological advantage they had if the neighboring tribes hear of this defeat. But it seems he is even more concerned for the Lord's name. If Israel fails God for any reason, it reflects on the great name of God. It will cause the people of the land to have less honor for the God Israel represents.

I hope by now you are starting to see the spiritual parallels to our battles. We have personal battles with our old nature and the temptations of the world. We have battles with the culture around us trying to suppress the truth of Jesus. We have battles with the forces of darkness that would deter us from letting Jesus shine through us and have us settle for less than God has for us. But if we give in, what will God do for His great name? In our grief we forget that God is more than capable of defending His name. The reality is that this defeat *was* defending the holiness of His name.

We have the incredible privilege of representing the Creator of the universe. But when we misrepresent Him, like the Achan did by taking in Jericho's polluted things, we are sending the wrong message. We are saying that our God is not so different from other gods and that He doesn't really change our lives that much. Our message becomes mixed and confusing. The result is people thinking less of Jesus.

If we will really be separate from worldliness like we talked about in the last lesson from Joshua, if we will not compromise with the polluted things and will serve people in love, letting the life of Christ be manifest in our mortal bodies (Romans 8:11), then people will be drawn to Jesus. We will gain ground for the kingdom of God. No walls or gates will be able to withstand our assault on evil to rescue the souls of men (Matthew 6:18). All things work together for good to those who are called according to God's good purposes (Romans 8:28). Even defeat is a blessing from God to turn our hearts and minds toward Him to seek His will.

But now let me turn to our nation. The polluted things are no longer recognized as being polluted. In fact, they are lauded (Isaiah 5:20). Our entertainment and educational systems have perverted our culture's perspective. We would like to blame our leaders, but nations get the leaders they deserve. While we love this nation and its original principles of a balance of power and equal representation, to be judged by our peers, and that moral principles be honored and laws obeyed, we see that rapidly slipping away. Isn't it fascinating that the army of Israel was defeated by a city spelled AI? Our over-confidence and greed has led to some major defeats. The watering down of the truth of Scripture and the outright mocking of it by so many tells us we are no longer the nation we once were.

The only answer to spiritual defeat is the one we see in this passage. There must be a humbling before the Lord like Joshua and the elders humbled themselves before God, and I'm afraid that will only happen in desperation. But remember church, we are citizens of heaven (Ephesians 2:19). We can humble ourselves before the Lord and the church can rise up victorious despite the culture in which it exists. That is what happened in Rome. The culture was collapsing, and the nation was splintering, but the church was gaining ground. We serve the same almighty God today!

A hymn calls to us. *Rise up oh men of God. Have done with lesser things. Give heart and soul and mind and strength to serve the King of kings. Rise up o men of God, the church for you doth wait, her strength unequal to her task, rise up and make her great!* And the way to rise up is to fall down on our faces before God, to rid our lives of the polluted things. James 1:27 tells us, *27 Religion that is pure and undefiled before God, the Father, is this: to visit orphans and widows in their affliction, and to keep oneself unstained from the world.* Let us put away the polluted things from our midst. Let us love God with all our heart, soul, mind, and strength (Matthew 22:37). Let us look to the leading of the Word and the Holy Spirit instead of our natural tendencies and so-called good ideas. It is then that *His life* in us will serve those in need, shine light in the darkness, and overcome the spiritual walls that must come down for the kingdom of God to advance in the hearts of mankind. Jesus promised that if we are standing on Him as our rock of truth, the gates of hell will not withstand our assault (Matthew 16:18).

Questions:

1 Review what has happened so far in Joshua.
2 What is the cycle of nations?
3 Why was the nation affected by one man's sin?
4 Why do we suffer from the sins of others?
5 What was the first mistake regarding Ai?
6 How did Joshua respond?
7 Who was to blame?
8 Why is there no back armor?
9 What was Joshua's concern?
10 How does that relate to our lives?

Deal with It! Joshua 7:10-26

Last week we read of the defeat of Israel at Ai. Something was terribly wrong. The fear that had gripped the hedonistic nations in the Promised Land (2:9), now gripped the nation of Israel (7:5). The miraculous victory over Jericho was followed by the sobering defeat at the little city of Ai. Joshua fell on his face in mourning and prayer over the 36 men who died in the battle. Moses and the people and the LORD Himself had told Joshua to be strong and courageous (1:9). Instead of doing that, he was whining. Whenever we are whining and dejected it is because things didn't go like we wanted. Dejection is not anyone's fault but our own. It is a result of our demands upon others or upon God are not met. We demand an answer from God instead of seeking God's heart in the matter.

Israel had turned and run when they saw that God was not with them. It was a painful lesson. Today's passage reveals why and gives us some spiritual truths that are applicable in our day.

{}^{10} The LORD said to Joshua, "Get up! Why have you fallen on your face? {}^{11} Israel has sinned; they have transgressed my covenant that I commanded them; they

*have taken some of the devoted things; they have stolen
and lied and put them among their own belongings. ¹²
Therefore the people of Israel cannot stand before their
enemies. They turn their backs before their enemies,
because they have become devoted for destruction. I will
be with you no more, unless you destroy the devoted things
from among you.* Joshua 7:10-12 The LORD told him,
"Get up!" He asked Joshua what he was doing on his face.
And then explained to Joshua the reason for the defeat.
Once again, the wording implies the whole nation is
affected because of one man's sin. "Israel has sinned."

God revealed to Joshua the reason for the defeat
was disobedience, for they had "taken," "stolen," and
"lied." All these actions were a transgression of the
covenant they had just renewed (Genesis 17:8)! Someone
had taken from the things devoted to destruction.

If God is to be our God, then we are to be obedient.
As someone once said, saying "No Lord!" is an oxymoron.
When there is disobedience God cannot bless us. When the
cursed things of the world are among us, we cannot stand
before our adversary. In that condition we should fear to
stand before God. God does not desert us as He did with
their army (Hebrews 13:5), but we will not go forward in
victory. If they did not deal with the sin in the camp, God
would not go with them. God was holding them to the
same standard that He held their enemies. Prior to the
battle of Jericho, He told Joshua He is not taking sides
(5:14).

If you wonder why, you have not been victorious in
your Christian walk, this may give you a possible answer.
Whatever it is that is of this world, lust of the eyes, lust of
the flesh, and the pride of life, needs to be forsaken (1 John
2:15-17). Get rid of it! Destroy it. Be severe. Jesus said
that if your eye causes you to sin, it is better to pluck out
your eye than to be cast into hell with both eyes (Matthew

5:29). Be holy, for the One who is with you is holy (1 Peter 1:15,16).

Jesus died to sanctify us so that we could be vessels of the Holy Spirit and have the power of His presence flow through our lives (John 14:23). If we then cling to that which is unholy, dedicated to destruction, then we are intentionally cutting ourselves off from His enabling power. We deny ourselves of the intimacy we could have with Him. We dare not stand before God's throne in prayer while clinging to some detestable thing.

Why does God hate evil to such an extent? It is because He loves what is good to such an extent. Love of what is good necessitates abhorring what is evil. God loves us and He knows the damage evil does to us. He tells us that if we love Him, we should hate evil like He does (Psalm 97:10). When He commands us to love Him with our all, He is telling us to love what is good. It is not because He is on an ego trip. It is because He wants us to love what is good, holy, righteous, and true.

13 Get up! Consecrate the people and say, 'Consecrate yourselves for tomorrow; for thus says the LORD, God of Israel, "There are devoted things in your midst, O Israel. You cannot stand before your enemies until you take away the devoted things from among you." Joshua 7:13 So what do we do about our condition? Quit laying on your face praying and complaining to God. Get up and consecrate yourself anew. Remember that they consecrated themselves before they crossed the Jordan (3:5). Throw away the vile things that have stolen your heart away from God. Is it pornography, or a lust, or drugs, or anything that God has told you to forsake? If you refuse to surrender it, you will not be able to be victorious in your daily walk with Christ. Once it is removed, you can consecrate your life again to God. Intimacy is restored

(Zechariah 1:3). The power of the Holy Spirit is present, and the life of Christ can flow through you again.

What follows is God's plan to expose the sin in the camp. Sometimes we need God's revelation as to how to free ourselves from the things devoted to destruction. But usually, it is simply forsaking it with the help of God. Some people can't own a computer or TV because of the temptation. Others have to stop going to certain locations like the liquor aisle. Sometimes it just means sell the thing that is taking up all your time and use that time to be in prayer and the Word. But in every case, the battle is for our minds and hearts. We must expose the lie of Satan that tells us its ok because your particular disobedience is not that bad. He tells us no one else will get hurt and you need this. But as we have seen, each of us affects everyone else in the body of Christ (Ephesians 4:25).

14 In the morning therefore you shall be brought near by your tribes. And the tribe that the LORD takes by lot shall come near by clans. And the clan that the LORD takes shall come near by households. And the household that the LORD takes shall come near man by man. 15 And he who is taken with the devoted things shall be burned with fire, he and all that he has, because he has transgressed the covenant of the LORD, and because he has done an outrageous thing in Israel.'" Joshua 7:14,15 God was going to point out the man who had rebelled against His command. I imagine when Achan heard what was about to take place he tried to sneak off, but someone must have seen him. How his heart must have pounded as his tribe was chosen, then his clan, and finally his household. The devoted things were to be burned with fire. Now the one who had chosen to take them had in effect made himself and all that was his a part of those things devoted to destruction.

Achan's act was outrageous because it was done after such an amazing miracle that followed the covenant renewal (5:2). Obviously, God was present in the parting of Jordan and the overthrow of Jericho. And the only wall standing was Rahab's house. Amazing! And therefore, it was outrageous that someone would that day defy the God to whom just days before they had pledged to be holy. But is it any less outrageous that we who know of the life, death, and resurrection of Jesus and enter the New Covenant to be holy vessels to the Lord and yet still defy His commands (John 14:15)?

This rebellion reminds me of the first sin. Adam and Eve had everything they could want, a perfect environment, a perfect spouse, and God walking with them in the Garden, speaking directly to them. There was only one thing that was forbidden, the tree of the knowledge of good and evil (Genesis 2:16,17). One must have the option to choose love, or it is forced. Adam and Eve did not know what evil was. Choosing to disobey the only command opened their eyes to evil and from then on there was a distinction between good and evil. No longer was their instinct to do good. They could then choose to do good or evil at every turn. And sadly, we inherited that condition. Achan chose to do evil, and it affected the nation like Adam and Eve's sin affected the world (Romans 5:12).

16 So Joshua rose early in the morning and brought Israel near tribe by tribe, and the tribe of Judah was taken. 17 And he brought near the clans of Judah, and the clan of the Zerahites was taken. And he brought near the clan of the Zerahites man by man, and Zabdi was taken. 18 And he brought near his household man by man, and Achan the son of Carmi, son of Zabdi, son of Zerah, of the tribe of Judah, was taken. Joshua 7:16-18 When Joshua got the instructions as to how to deal with Jericho he rose early to obey. Now there is another battle, an internal one, and he has the same eagerness to obey. This internal battle of the spirit was going on during the battle of Jericho within Achan's heart. Now Joshua is aware of it. While one battle was won, another was lost, and it manifested in the defeat at Ai. God made the nation aware so the rebellion would not spread like cancer throughout the nation.

The choices were made by lots. That is when stones are marked and put in a jar that is shaken until one stone is pulled out or falls out randomly. This took man's influence out of the picture and left it up to God (Proverbs 16:33). It showed God was in charge of each choice. It also showed the people that it wasn't human discovery, but the all-seeing God who was exposing sin. Nothing is hidden from His sight (Hebrews 4:13). It put a healthy fear of God in the congregation.

This event reminds me of when Jesus told those at the Last Supper that one of them would betray Him (Matthew 26:21). It causes everyone to examine their hearts. Is my heart wholly dedicated to God and His service? Have I really been obedient (2 Corinthians 13:5)? Is there an ounce of selfish betrayal in my heart?

19 Then Joshua said to Achan, "My son, give glory to the LORD God of Israel and give praise to him. And tell me now what you have done; do not hide it from me." Joshua 7:19 This phrase, "give glory to the LORD God of Israel and give praise to him," became an oath commanding people to confess before God. It is probably the oath the Pharisees commanded over the man born blind who was healed in John 9:24. It would also have been the oath the high priest commanded of Jesus in Matthew 26:63. They said, "Tell us the truth; are you the Son of God?" Jesus then said, "You say that I AM." And then Jesus quoted a passage from the prophet Daniel that says all the world will worship Him (Daniel 7:13,14; Psalm 110:1). Jesus honored the oath.

20 And Achan answered Joshua, "Truly I have sinned against the LORD God of Israel, and this is what I did: 21 when I saw among the spoil a beautiful cloak from Shinar, and 200 shekels of silver, and a bar of gold weighing 50 shekels, then I coveted them and took them. And see, they are hidden in the earth inside my tent, with the silver underneath." Joshua 7:20,21 "I saw ... I coveted ... [I] took ... they are hidden." Here is exactly the same anatomy of temptation and sin that we witnessed in mankind's first great disobedience in the fall.[x] When Achan broke the tenth commandment to not covet, he went on to break the eighth to not steal (Romans 7:7,8). His theft was of things that were to be in the temple treasury. It was God who gave the victory. The spoils belonged to God. He literally stole from God because he had another god – material things! That was breaking the first commandment (Exodus 20:3).

We have all experienced the same conflict within. God tells us not to do something. We see it. Desire grows. Then we act on it in disobedience to God who loved us and gave Himself for us. Thank God for the Holy Spirit who convicts us before we give in to desire. He satisfies our hungry hearts when we take time with Him (Psalm 107:9). Then the Babylonian robes, or silver, or gold cannot compete for our desires.

He hid these objects in his tent. When did he think he could get away with wearing that robe? Wouldn't someone ask him where he got it? Sin is often so unreasonable. The very possession of a thing will not bring joy. Instead, it brings worry that someone will find out. It brings guilt that we have disobeyed. Is there something hidden in your tent?

The Bible compares our bodies to tents (2 Corinthians 5:4), and sometimes there is something hidden inside, in our hearts, some lust that we secretly wish for.

The lie of Satan is that having that thing will make you truly happy. And then the opportunity comes, and you take possession of it and find out it is a quickly fading pleasure that doesn't measure up to your expectation. The consequences are more costly than you could have imagined.

We should have learned that lesson from our childhood. Each Christmas there is such excitement as we rip off the wrapping paper and find our wish granted. But before long the thing is in the closet and we are hoping for our birthday gift. Substitutes for God never last. They never live up to the promise. And often, as in Achan's case, they end in destruction.

22 So Joshua sent messengers, and they ran to the tent; and behold, it was hidden in his tent with the silver underneath. 23 And they took them out of the tent and brought them to Joshua and to all the people of Israel. And they laid them down before the LORD. Joshua 7:22,23 The evidence was revealed. The enemy's lie is often, "No one will ever know," but the Scriptures declare, "Be sure your sin will find you out" (Numbers 32:23).

24 And Joshua and all Israel with him took Achan the son of Zerah, and the silver and the cloak and the bar of gold, and his sons and daughters and his oxen and donkeys and sheep and his tent and all that he had. And they brought them up to the Valley of Achor. 25 And Joshua said, "Why did you bring trouble on us? The LORD brings trouble on you today." And all Israel stoned him with stones. They burned them with fire and stoned them with stones. 26 And they raised over him a great heap of stones that remains to this day. Then the LORD turned from his burning anger. Therefore, to this day the name of that place is called the Valley of Achor. Joshua 7:24-26 Thirty-six men died because of Achan's sin. He made his family and possessions part of the things devoted to destruction.

As far as we know He never pleaded for mercy. Achor means trouble. The valley was called trouble to remind them and us that when we rebel against God, we not only bring trouble on our family, but on those with whom we are a part. No man is an island. We all affect one another. The Apostle wrote *26 If one member suffers, all suffer together; if one member is honored, all rejoice together.* 1 Corinthians 12:26

Holiness was restored. Sin was removed. Now the nation could continue to take the land and see the fulfillment of the ancient promise. What a gripping warning is presented to us in this account! The New Testament church is not a theocracy like Israel. We don't try to hunt out sin in the congregation, but often God will expose it. There is such a thing as church discipline (1 Corinthians 5:9-11) and restoration (Galatians 6:1). No matter how one tries, sin cannot remain hidden.

In the beginning of the church something similar happened. It is recorded in Acts 5:1-11. The church was off to an amazing start with the pouring out of the Spirit and miracles witnessed by all. But one couple plotted to lie to the Apostles and to the Holy Spirit. They died as a result. It wasn't about the gift or the amount they held back; it was their intentional act of deceit. How God's justice calls us to a holy life! Jesus warned us, *15 And he said to them, "Take care, and be on your guard against all covetousness, for one's life does not consist in the abundance of his possessions."* Luke 12:15 Realize how our lives affect others. The more we have seen of God's miraculous works and the more we know of His Word, the more accountable we are (Luke 12:48).

By the grace of God let us be a blessing to the body of Christ and our family, and the community in which we live. Let us have lives that are joyfully obedient to our LORD because of His eternal covenant with us. Let us find our satisfaction in Him and His Word so that nothing can compete for our desires. Let us help one another do battle in this internal war of the spiritual realm that turns our eyes from Jesus and loving one another to greed and selfishness.

We all deserve Achan's fate, for we have all coveted worldly things and been disobedient. But that is why Jesus came. God is ruthless with sin because He is holy, and He loves us. Sin is destructive to us. Its earned wages are death (Romans 3:23). But in mercy and love Jesus took the punishment we deserved.

Instead of looking at a pile of stones and remembering Achan and his disobedience, we look at a cross and remember His obedience that brought us the mercy and grace of God. We become ruthless with sin in our own lives, not because we fear judgment, but because we realize what this New Covenant cost the One who sealed it with His own blood. Instead of the valley of Achor, which means trouble, we have the hill of Calvary that is our spiritual place of victory, where we died to our old self with Jesus (Romans 6:3). We look to the empty tomb and claim that resurrection life in Him (Colossians 2:12). As we keep Jesus first in our lives, let us go in and take the land by bringing souls of men and women to our Savior, Christ Jesus the King!

Questions:
1 Why was Joshua so dejected?
2 Why did they lose the battle?
3 What are some of the devoted things today?
4 Why does God hate evil?
5 What battle is always raging?
6 Who sealed Achan's fate?
7 Who did Achan rob?
8 Can things bring lasting joy?
9 Can sin remain hidden?

10 Why should we be ruthless against sin in our own life?

Victory and Renewal Joshua 8

The spiritual analogy we saw in the previous chapter where Ai defeated Israel in battle was that when we have clung to the wicked things in this world, the Lord will not help us fight our spiritual battles. Compromise handicaps our spiritual lives. We need to turn to the Lord to know how to get back on track.

Now that the compromise was dealt with and the things devoted to destruction were burned and buried, Israel was ready to continue the conquest of the land. When we confess and forsake our sins, the Lord goes before us and helps us fight our spiritual battles. We saw how important it is for us to forsake the evil things in our own lives.

[1] And the LORD said to Joshua, "Do not fear and do not be dismayed. Take all the fighting men with you, and arise, go up to Ai. See, I have given into your hand the king of Ai, and his people, his city, and his land. Joshua 8:1 Joshua is encouraged by the LORD to not fear or be dismayed. The word in Hebrew for dismayed means broken down or fall apart. In other words, quit being afraid, buck up, and get it together. That is how we begin to get back on track. We should not wallow in our failures, but we should repent and turn to the Lord for His directions (Romans 8:1).

Most importantly God told Joshua the city has been given to him, past tense, done deal! We can know that the Lord has given us the victory too. It was already won on the cross. We can wallow in our past, but God says to us what He said to Joshua, "Get up! Stop being fearful. Get yourself together!" Deal with the sin. Get rid of the unclean things and start walking in the power of the Spirit.

112

Claim the resurrection power of Jesus to empower you to say no to sin and yes to His will. Know that the battle before you is already won!

As with Jericho, the LORD gave Joshua the battle plan. He was to lay an ambush behind the city. Apparently, there were more details given as we see in verse 8. Some of our weaknesses also need battle plans. What verse will you memorize to counter a temptation or bad habit? Who will you ask to keep you accountable? Whatever the Lord directs you to do, do it!

God rarely has us do the same thing twice. That is because we would end up following the method instead of looking to the Lord. If every time Jesus healed someone He put mud over their eyes, we would have a "mud over eyes" ministry. It would teach what mud to use, how to make it, how to apply it, and where to have the person wash it out. However, there is only one method that always works. Ask the LORD for direction and do what He says.

² And you shall do to Ai and its king as you did to Jericho and its king. Only its spoil and its livestock you shall take as plunder for yourselves. Lay an ambush against the city, behind it." Joshua 8:2 This time the spoils of war would belong to the soldiers. Manna is no longer falling, and they need to feed their families. As was the case with Jericho, no one was to survive. I explained why that was a necessity in the previous sermon. In brief, it was because of the culture's 400 years of increasing depravity.

³ So Joshua and all the fighting men arose to go up to Ai. And Joshua chose 30,000 mighty men of valor and sent them out by night. ⁴ And he commanded them, "Behold, you shall lie in ambush against the city, behind it. Do not go very far from the city, but all of you remain ready. ⁵ And I and all the people who are with me will approach the city. And when they come out against us just as before, we shall flee before them. ⁶ And they will come *out after us, until we have drawn them away from the city. For they will say, 'They are fleeing from us, just as before.' So we will flee before them. ⁷ Then you shall rise up from the ambush and seize the city, for the LORD your God will give it into your hand.* Joshua 8:3-7 This time Joshua took a much larger army. He sent 30,000 men on a night march to Ai and hid to the west of the city. He took the smaller group to encamp on the north side of the city with a ravine between them and the city. This would be the battle force the king of Ai would see in the morning.

The plan was to draw the army of Ai out after the smaller group as they retreated. If all went well, the men of the city would also come out hoping for spoils of war when they saw the Israelites retreat. That would leave the city open to attack. Then Joshua would signal the hidden forces to attack the city. The smoke from the city burning would frighten and confound Ai's forces as they would realize they could not retreat to the city's walls.

In the morning, the king of Ai ordered his army to attack. Israel retreated, which encouraged all the men still holding the city and the men of a nearby town, Bethel, to leave the cities and pursue them. The plan worked just as intended. The city was completely defenseless to the soldiers who were hidden. I am going to skip over the battle details and go on to verse 18.

¹⁸ Then the LORD said to Joshua, "Stretch out the javelin that is in your hand toward Ai, for I will give it into your hand." And Joshua stretched out the javelin that was in his hand toward the city. Joshua 8:18 Apparently there was a prearranged signal that when Joshua held his javelin toward Ai, the hidden forces were to attack the city. The LORD spoke to Joshua to tell him the best moment and repeated His promise that He had given Israel the city. Joshua gave the signal.

The hidden troops quickly set fire to the city so that the army of Ai would see their city was taken. This would have caused them to panic, knowing they had been tricked. The men with Joshua turned around and attacked. The troops in the city attacked and the forces of Ai were trapped in between and slaughtered. The only one left alive was the King of Ai. Now skipping down to verse 24.

24 When Israel had finished killing all the inhabitants of Ai in the open wilderness where they pursued them, and all of them to the very last had fallen by the edge of the sword, all Israel returned to Ai and struck it down with the edge of the sword. 25 And all who fell that day, both men and women, were 12,000, all the people of Ai. Joshua 8:24-25 Once the battle was over, the entire population of Ai was killed, a total of 12,000 people. Yes, this was genocide, but not because of their race, but because God's judgment of their vile lives. If you have not read the reason for this in previous sermons in Joshua please go back and read of the justice and patience of God and the barbarity of that civilization that was devoted to destruction.

It is a foreshadow of the Great White Throne judgment when all of mankind will be held accountable for their rebellion against the goodness of God (Revelation 20:15; 21:8). To say God is barbaric is to ignore the wickedness of these people and the need for God to be just. The problem with all of man's systems is injustice. In numerous Bible passages judges were told to be impartial and to refuse to accept bribes (Exodus 18:21). We are unjust toward others because of the selfishness and greed that are part of our fallen nature. The only remedy is Christ who changes our hearts.

26 But Joshua did not draw back his hand with which he stretched out the javelin until he had devoted all the inhabitants of Ai to destruction. Joshua 8:26 Joshua kept his javelin stretched out toward Ai until they had done all the LORD commanded them to do. Perhaps he remembered how Moses' arms were held up by Aaron and Hur when he fought the Amalekites . As long as Moses held the banner high, they were victorious (Exodus 17:10,11). The LORD told Joshua to stretch it out, and so he obeyed until all was accomplished.

Sometimes we hear what God wants us to do and we begin to obey. But after the main thing seems almost done, we slack off and never fully finish. Partial obedience is not really obedience. Joshua understood that. His stretched-out javelin was a sign to the army to finish what they had begun. This reminds us to persevere in our spiritual battles until we are home in glory. Do not be weary in doing God's good will, for in due season you will prevail if you do not quit (Galatians 6:9)

I have seen many begin to follow the Lord and in time they settled for the world and what it has to offer. Sometimes the most excited new believer falls the hardest because he or she finds the cost was more than they were expecting. That is why we must count the cost and decide if we are in this to the end because Jesus took it to the end for us (Luke 14:27,28).

27 Only the livestock and the spoil of that city Israel took as their plunder, according to the word of the LORD that he commanded Joshua. 28 So Joshua burned Ai and made it forever a heap of ruins, as it is to this day. Joshua 8:27-28 While Jericho and all things in it were devoted to destruction, the LORD gave permission for the army to take the spoils from the city of Ai. Once the city was plundered and burned, the walls were toppled to make it a ruined heap.

29 And he hanged the king of Ai on a tree until evening. And at sunset Joshua commanded, and they took his body down from the tree and threw it at the entrance of the gate of the city and raised over it a great heap of stones, which stands there to this day. Joshua 8:29 The king was hanged on a tree and left until evening. The Law told them whoever was hanged on a tree was cursed (Deuteronomy 21:23). Then his body was thrown at the entrance of the city and rocks were piled high over it. When the author recorded the account, the pile of stones was still in place. This foreshadows Satan's final demise when he and his angels are thrown into the Lake of Fire.

The Old Testament foreshadowing is seen supremely in the prophecy of Isaiah, written as an extended answer to the question posed in his opening chapter. How can the faithless city (Jerusalem) become the faithful city (the new Jerusalem)? Or to put it in more universal terms, how is the sinful human race ever to be rescued, redeemed, and restored to the image of God in which we were created? Isaiah's answer is given in the three portraits of the Messiah as the incarnate Son, God with us, Emmanuel (Isaiah 1-39), the suffering servant (Isaiah 40-55), and the warrior king or the anointed conqueror (Isaiah 56-66). The last of the three figures is especially significant here. In Isaiah 63:1-6 the portrait is drawn of a mysterious figure clothed in splendid apparel, but his garments are red-stained not with the vintage of the trodden grapes but with the lifeblood of the nations, trampled in his wrath. This is "the day of vengeance of our God" (Isaiah 61:2). If there is no ultimate destruction of all God's enemies, there can be no guarantee of the ultimate inviolability of his eternal kingdom of love, joy, and peace. The opposition has to be vanquished and removed if the kingdom of God is to rule as the new creation. So the picture of the king of Ai hanging on a tree until evening, gruesome as it is, conveys the reminder that the same destruction ultimately awaits all God's enemies, "for our God is a consuming fire" (Hebrews 12:29). Or in

Paul's words, "Then comes the end, when [Christ] delivers the kingdom to God the Father after destroying every rule and every authority and power. For he must reign until he has put all his enemies under his feet. The last enemy to be destroyed is death" (1 Corinthians 15:24-26). This is the logical necessity if there is to be an everlasting kingdom, a holy city, the new Jerusalem, where death shall be no more and where there will be no mourning or crying or pain or tears (see Revelation 21:1-4).[xi]-David Jackman

If you are saddened that there will be those who forever refuse the goodness and love of God, you share God's heart. He is not willing that any should perish (2 Peter 3:9). But God will not force anyone to repent, nor will He allow anyone who refuses His mercy to corrupt our heavenly home with their rebellious presence.

After the victory, the nation moved northward to fulfill a command God gave through Moses. *[30] At that time Joshua built an altar to the LORD, the God of Israel, on Mount Ebal, [31] just as Moses the servant of the LORD had commanded the people of Israel, as it is written in the Book of the Law of Moses, "an altar of uncut stones, upon which no man has wielded an iron tool." And they offered on it burnt offerings to the LORD and sacrificed peace offerings.* Joshua 8:30-31 Joshua was told in chapter one verse eight to be careful to do all that is written in the Law (Joshua 1:8). He was to obey the commands God gave to Moses. We find the commands of what they were to do when they crossed the Jordan in Deuteronomy 27:4-8: *[4] And when you have crossed over the Jordan, you shall set up these stones, concerning which I command you today, on Mount Ebal, and you shall plaster them with plaster. [5] And there you shall build an altar to the LORD your God, an altar of stones. You shall wield no iron tool on them; [6] you shall build an altar to the LORD your God of uncut stones. And you shall offer burnt offerings on it to the LORD your God, ⁷ and you shall sacrifice peace offerings and shall eat there, and you shall rejoice before the LORD your God. ⁸ And you shall write on the stones all the words of this law very plainly.*

Burnt offerings were the sacrifice of an unblemished male bull, sheep, or bird, depending on the financial ability of the one bringing the offering. It was to atone for their sin. Atone means to cover sin. It does not mean to remove it. Only Jesus' blood could remove our sins (Hebrews 10:4). The person bringing the offering would place his hand on the head of the animal before it was slain. This pictured repentance and the transfer of sins so that the penalty of death was upon the animal. Of course, this was only a picture of how Jesus would come and take our sins upon Himself and the punishment of death that our sins deserved. (See Leviticus 1.) There had been Achan's sin of breaking the covenant and Israel's self-directed attack on Ai resulting in loss of 36 lives. That is why the sin offering came first. That could then be followed by the peace offering, also known as the fellowship offering. The peace offering is described in Leviticus 4. It was a celebration that peace between them and God had been restored (Leviticus 7:29-34).

It is significant that they were given the animals from the city of Ai. So, it was really God who provided their sacrifices, just as He would provide the ultimate sacrifice.

³² And there, in the presence of the people of Israel, he wrote on the stones a copy of the law of Moses, which he had written. Joshua 8:32 Deuteronomy 27:2-4 tells us that these uncut stones were to be covered in plaster. Since no tool could mark the stones the law would have been written on the plaster over the stones. The book of the law

119

of Moses would cover Exodus 20 through chapter 23 which includes the Ten Commandments.

33 And all Israel, sojourner as well as native born, with their elders and officers and their judges, stood on opposite sides of the ark before the Levitical priests who carried the ark of the covenant of the LORD, half of them in front of Mount Gerizim and half of them in front of Mount Ebal, just as Moses the servant of the LORD had commanded at the first, to bless the people of Israel. 34 And afterward he read all the words of the law, the blessing and the curse, according to all that is written in the Book of the Law. 35 There was not a word of all that Moses commanded that Joshua did not read before all the assembly of Israel, and the women, and the little ones, and the sojourners who lived among them. Joshua 8:33-35 This was the perfect place for the recitation. The mountain formations form perfect amphitheaters. The direction God gave Moses was to build the altar on Mt. Ebal (Deuteronomy 27:4), the mountain where the curses are recited. This altar was recently discovered on Mount Ebal.

Israel was divided into two groups, one on Gerazim and the other on Ebal with the ark of the covenant and the Levitical priests who carried the ark in the valley of Shechem between the two mountains. Joshua read the blessings for obeying the law and the curses for disobeying it. Deuteronomy 11:29 tells us the tribes on Gerazim, a wooded and fruitful mountain, would repeat the blessings and the tribes on Ebal, a barren rocky mountain, would repeat the curses (Deuteronomy 27:12,13). This would have included Deuteronomy 28 which lists the blessings and curses. The altar on top of the mountain of curses signified atoning sacrifices saving us from the just judgments of God.

The people were taking the land, and these laws with their blessings, and curses were to be their guide as to how to live as a nation. Because of their recent failure, it was the perfect time to renew their covenant with God. I wonder what their future would have been had they done this on a yearly basis. During the life of Joshua, they did obey (Joshua 24:31), but not long after Joshua's death, they began to do what was right in their own eyes (Judges 17:6). They forgot the barren picture that Mount Ebal presented. We forget it today. A life in obedience to Jesus' commands and walking in the Spirit will be fruitful (Psalm 1:2,3). A life lived for the flesh will be a barren waste (Galatians 6:8).

We have the same challenge of reading the blessings in God's promises that we have in Jesus. We also have the warnings from Israel's history, the New Testament authors, and from Jesus (Matthew 7:24-27). Are we reading them often and taking heed to them? Whenever we read the New Testament, we will come across blessings, the greatest of which is forgiveness of sins and eternal life with our Savior (Ephesians 1:7). The ultimate curse comes from our rejection of the Holy Spirit drawing us to Jesus (John 6:44). That curse is eternal judgment. These blessings and curses are infinitely greater than those they recited on the Gerazim and Ebal. Shouldn't we remind ourselves each day of what has been revealed to us in the Word?

Let us end the message today by doing what they did but with promises and curses given to us in the New Covenant. Those to my right please read the promise on the screen and when they are finished those on the left read the curse. Let us stand and recite them together.

Promise - John 3:36 (ESV) [36a] Whoever believes in the Son has eternal life;
Curse - [36b] whoever does not obey the Son shall not see life, but the wrath of God remains on him.

Promise.-.Romans 2:6-8 (ESV) [6] He will render to each one according to his works: [7] to those who by patience in well-doing seek for glory and honor and immortality, he will give eternal life;

Curse- [8] but for those who are self-seeking and do not obey the truth, but obey unrighteousness, there will be wrath and fury

Promise - - Revelation 7:17 (ESV)

[17] For the Lamb in the midst of the throne will be their shepherd, and he will guide them to springs of living water, and God will wipe away every tear from their eyes."

Curse - Luke 21:34 (ESV)

[34] "But watch yourselves lest your hearts be weighed down with dissipation and drunkenness and cares of this life, and that day come upon you suddenly like a trap.

Promise - Mark 9:41 (ESV)

[41] For truly, I say to you, whoever gives you a cup of water to drink because you belong to Christ will by no means lose his reward.

Curse - Romans 2:5 (ESV)

[5] But because of your hard and impenitent heart you are storing up wrath for yourself on the day of wrath when God's righteous judgment will be revealed.

Does that give you a little sense of what it would have been like? We need reminders to walk in victory, to refuse compromise, and to give us regular reality checks. Let me close with pronouncing a benediction of praise to God for giving us the truth of His Word.

Romans 11:33-36 *[33] Oh, the depth of the riches and wisdom and knowledge of God! How unsearchable are his judgments and how inscrutable his ways! [34] "For who has known the mind of the Lord, or who has been his counselor?" [35] "Or who has given a gift to him that he might be repaid?" [36] For from him and through him and to him are all things. To him be glory forever. Amen.*

Questions:

1 What had happened previously that cleared the way for God to help them?

2 How do we know our battle is already won?

3 How do we prepare for our battles?

4 What does the destruction of Ai foreshadow?

5 Why did Joshua keep his javelin stretched out?

6 Why must God's enemies be defeated and judged?

7 What two sacrifices were offered? Why in that order?

8 How did the condition of the mountains convey the message?

9 Did reciting those verses give you a sense of what it was like?

10 Will you remember the declarations in God's Word daily?

Glorious Surrender! Joshua 9

Israel had just learned a hard lesson when the town of Ai killed thirty-six of their soldiers. They learned another lesson when Joshua complained to God about the defeat. They had not listened to God before the attack on Ai, nor did they ask God the reason for their defeat. Once sin was cleared from the camp and they heard from God on how to proceed, they were victorious. But the lesson of hearing from God first was still not learned. Our passage today drives it home a third time. As we go over it, we should consider how mankind is so prone to acting without prayer or seeking God's direction.

¹ As soon as all the kings who were beyond the Jordan in the hill country and in the lowland all along the coast of the Great Sea toward Lebanon, the Hittites, the Amorites, the Canaanites, the Perizzites, the Hivites, and the Jebusites, heard of this, ² they gathered together as one to fight against Joshua and Israel. Joshua 9:1,2 This is the first of two main coalitions that attempt to stop Israel from taking the land promised to them by God (11:1,2). Remember that God held off His judgment of this land for 400 years until the cup of the iniquity of the Amorites was full (Genesis 15:16). That tells us the area was very wicked. They had the King of Righteousness in the days of Abraham who surely proclaimed the way of God. But over the 400 years they had become so wicked that their extermination was the only way to end the evil and keep it from infecting Israel. Because they were so attuned to evil, they were open to Satan's influence to try to stop Israel instead of asking for a treaty. One could say they were only trying to protect their land, but we should not forget that they were determined to continue in their wickedness and were led by Satan as much as Israel was led by God. This spiritual battle with its long history (Daniel 10:13) manifests in our day as antisemitism.

We have already noticed that Israel's battle in the physical has many parallels to our battles in the spiritual realm. They began claiming the Promised Land by miraculously crossing the Jordan River and circumcising the men. That pictures the beginning of new life in Christ. Then they listened to the LORD's direction and started with the miraculous conquest of Jericho. That is our honeymoon time when it seems God takes such special care of us as baby Christians. Then compromise entered via Achan's greed, and they experienced defeat at Ai. That is our stumbling back into the old life and God's discipline. But after that, there is repentance and dependence on God again which brought victory. And so it is with us.

Once those initial lessons were learned, they rededicated themselves to the covenant. And in our parallel, we regularly partake of communion and vow to surrender our lives to the LORD who gave Himself for us

(Titus 2:14). Then we are ready to take our spiritual heritage in Christ (Ephesians 2:6). That is when the enemy of our souls really takes notice and coordinates an attack to stop our progress in Christ. This is where we are at in our study of Joshua.

The Gibeonites heard of the conquest of Jericho and Ai, so they sought to save their lives. *³ But when the inhabitants of Gibeon heard what Joshua had done to Jericho and to Ai, ⁴ they on their part acted with cunning and went and made ready provisions and took worn-out sacks for their donkeys, and wineskins, worn-out and torn and mended, ⁵ with worn-out, patched sandals on their feet, and worn-out clothes. And all their provisions were dry and crumbly. ⁶ And they went to Joshua in the camp at Gilgal and said to him and to the men of Israel, "We have come from a distant country, so now make a covenant with us."* Joshua 9:3-6 Unlike the hard-hearted Canaanite coalition, the Gibeonites assessed the situation with reason. The Gibeonites, who were fierce warriors, realized that the God of Israel could not be defeated in war. Of all the people in the land, they were the only people group who, like Rahab, realized the God of Israel is undefeatable (2:11). They heard the amazing stories of the Israelite's deliverance from Egypt and their conquests. So, they relied on deception to save their lives. If the enemy cannot win by a frontal attack, he will try deception and compromise. He is subtle (Genesis 3:1). Why didn't the other groups come to the same realization? In this we can see that most people, even when faced with the evidence, will not surrender to the Lord even to save their lives (Matthew 7:13). Hardened hearts are without reason.

They prepared an elaborate deception by gathering everything they could find to give the appearance that they had come from a great distance, though they were really living nearby. It was a well-planned drama with all the right props. Every indication was that they had made a long journey. The deception was acted out. They asked Joshua to enter a covenant with them.

7 But the men of Israel said to the Hivites, "Perhaps you live among us; then how can we make a covenant with you?" Joshua 9:7 Initial concerns can come to mind because God brings them to mind. There was suspicion from the start that these people lived nearby. When we face important decisions, and we have a sense that something is not right, pray. Ask God for discernment. Take your time and check it out, especially when you desire a certain outcome. Our preferences can blind us to the truth. In the verses that follow notice how the leaders of Israel walk by sight and not by faith (Hebrews 11:6). See how flattery influences them to ignore their first concern.

8 They said to Joshua, "We are your servants." And Joshua said to them, "Who are you? And where do you come from?" 9 They said to him, "From a very distant country your servants have come, because of the name of the LORD your God. For we have heard a report of him, and all that he did in Egypt, 10 and all that he did to the two kings of the Amorites who were beyond the Jordan, to Sihon the king of Heshbon, and to Og king of Bashan, who lived in Ashtaroth. 11 So our elders and all the inhabitants of our country said to us, 'Take provisions in your hand for the journey and go to meet them and say to them, "We are your servants. Come now, make a covenant with us."' 12 Here is our bread. It was still warm when we took it from our houses as our food for the journey on the day we set out to come to you, but now, behold, it is dry and crumbly. 13 These wineskins were new when we filled them, and behold, they have burst. And these garments and sandals of ours are worn out from the very long journey." Joshua 9:8-12 They began by declaring to Joshua that they were his servants. So, Joshua asked them what people group they were of and where they came from. Notice how they never really answer his question specifically. They just said far away.

The only truth they told was the history of God's mighty acts on behalf of Israel. But they used this truth to back their lie. Deceit is often mixed with facts that are true. We think if one part is true it must all be true. But me thinks thou doth protest too much when they show the dry bread and cracked wineskins. It was a preplanned effort to try to convince Joshua they were telling the truth. "Look at our worn-out sandals!"

14 So the men took some of their provisions, but did not ask counsel from the LORD. Joshua 8:14 The men of Israel looked at the falsified evidence like Eve looked at the fruit (Genesis 3:6), like their parents looked at the giants (Numbers 13:33), and like Joshua first looked at Ai (7:3). They did not ask counsel from the LORD.

How did they cross the Jordan? How did they defeat Jericho? How did they defeat Ai? They asked counsel of the LORD. But this is different isn't it? They say they fear the name of the LORD. Even the demons fear the name of the LORD (James 2:19). Not everyone who tells you they honor Jesus is a follower of Jesus. I have met people who told me Jesus was their spirit guide. But that spirit did not guide them to the Word of God. Jesus is the Word incarnate (John 1:14). He consistently quoted and referred to Scripture. He chose the men who were to convey His message, and they quoted Scripture. He even said He was the fulfillment of all Scripture (Luke 24:44). So, if the Jesus you follow does not lead you to the Word of God, you are entertaining a spirit as deceptive as the Gibeonites (1 Timothy 4:1; Matthew 24:5).

Moses had told Joshua how to make important decisions. Numbers 27:18-21 *18 So the LORD said to Moses, "Take Joshua the son of Nun, a man in whom is the*

Spirit, and lay your hand on him. [19] Make him stand before Eleazar the priest and all the congregation, and you shall commission him in their sight. [20] You shall invest him with some of your authority, that all the congregation of the people of Israel may obey. [21] And he shall stand before Eleazar the priest, who shall inquire for him by the judgment of the Urim before the LORD. At his word they shall go out, and at his word they shall come in, both he and all the people of Israel with him, the whole congregation."

He was to go to the high priest and inquire of the LORD. But this situation appeared to be so obvious. Look at their clothes and provisions. Instead of listening to their first concerns, they listened to the Gibeonites well thought out deception and flattery. Did God not have them annihilate the people of the land because they were so evil? Then why would Joshua expect someone who might be from the land to tell the truth? Can you ask a liar if he or she is lying?

[15] And Joshua made peace with them and made a covenant with them, to let them live, and the leaders of the congregation swore to them. [16] At the end of three days after they had made a covenant with them, they heard that they were their neighbors and that they lived among them. [17] and the people of Israel set out and reached their cities on the third day. Now their cities were Gibeon, Chephirah, Beeroth, and Kiriath-jearim. Joshua 9:15-17 Surprise! We fooled you. The cities were just a few days away. The covenant could not be broken. Because they did not inquire of the LORD these people would remain in the land. The territory would not be taken. But we will see how God graciously redeemed the situation.

[18] But the people of Israel did not attack them, because the leaders of the congregation had sworn to them by the LORD, the God of Israel. Then all the congregation

murmured against the leaders. ¹⁹ But all the leaders said to all the congregation, "We have sworn to them by the LORD, the God of Israel, and now we may not touch them. ²⁰ This we will do to them: let them live, lest wrath be upon us, because of the oath that we swore to them." ²¹ And the leaders said to them, "Let them live." So they became cutters of wood and drawers of water for all the congregation, just as the leaders had said of them. Joshua 9:18-21The congregation rightly complained to the leaders, but it was too late. The sin of not getting counsel from God could not be made right by the sin of breaking their oath (Psalm 15:4). They had to keep their word, for their word represented the God of Israel. He does not break His covenants, so they should not break theirs even if it was made with deception. For better or worse, the world sees our actions as representing our God. Besides that, Moses had commanded that if any city opened their gates to Israel, the people could live but would become servants of Israel (Deuteronomy 20:10,11). The Gibeonites did fear the God of Israel.

This is a picture of the Lord's conquest of our hearts. If we resist His offer of peace, we will be conquered. If we accept it, we will serve Him. But serving Him is a wonderful gift for His yoke is easy and His burden is light (Matthew 11:28-30). The title servant of the Lord is an honorary title applied to prophets and kings.

Later in Israel's history, Israel will be judged by God because King Saul broke the covenant with the Gibeonites by attacking them. King David had to make reparations by handing over seven sons of Saul to be hung (2 Samuel 21:5,6). The Gibeonites did live as servants, just as they proclaimed.

²² Joshua summoned them, and he said to them, "Why did you deceive us, saying, 'We are very far from you,' when you dwell among us? ²³ Now therefore you are

cursed, and some of you shall never be anything but servants, cutters of wood and drawers of water for the house of my God." 24 They answered Joshua, "Because it was told to your servants for a certainty that the LORD your God had commanded his servant Moses to give you all the land and to destroy all the inhabitants of the land from before you—so we feared greatly for our lives because of you and did this thing. Joshua 9:22-24 "Why did you expect them to tell the truth?", would have been a better question for Joshua. Now the lesson of getting God's perspective, of walking by faith and not by sight is reinforced again (2 Corinthians 5:7). If Joshua is going to take all the land and win against the coalitions that gather against Israel, he must learn this crucial lesson.

If we are to lay up our treasures in heaven and fight the good fight of faith, we need to learn the same lesson (Matthew 6:19-21; 1 Timothy 6:12). We have a great high priest whose name is Jesus (Hebrews 4:14). He is always ready to guide us in our decisions so that we will be fruitful for the kingdom of God. He wants us to be victorious and not be deceived. That is why He gave us His Word and the Holy Spirit. These things happened to them as examples for us (1 Corinthians 10:6). Learn from their mistakes.

25 And now, behold, we are in your hand. Whatever seems good and right in your sight to do to us, do it." 26 So he did this to them and delivered them out of the hand of the people of Israel, and they did not kill them. 27 But Joshua made them that day cutters of wood and drawers of water for the congregation and for the altar of the LORD, to this day, in the place that he should choose. Joshua 9:25-27 The Gibeonites fear of the LORD caused Israel to accept their people including the future generations that would serve Israel. It is amazing to me that the Gibeonites remained a distinct people group even through the captivity in Babylon. When Nehemiah rebuilt the walls of Jerusalem, among the builders listed we find "Melatiah the Gibeonite and ... the men of Gibeon" (Nehemiah 3:7).

I think the Gibeonites did not have to use their elaborate deception. They could have opened their gates and pleaded for mercy and the outcome would have been the same. But Joshua and the leaders needed to learn a lesson that we all need to learn. *"Trust in the LORD with all your heart and lean not to your own understanding"* (See Proverbs 3:5,6). Walk by faith and not by sight. Do not judge with the sight of the eyes (Isaiah 11:3). Man looks on the outward appearances (1 Samuel 16:7). All these expressions we find woven throughout Scripture because we are so prone to leaning on our own understanding and judging by appearances (John 7:24). We need to learn to become God reliant instead of self-reliant.

Though the Gibeonites seem to be inspired by the subtle deceiver to infiltrate Israel with Canaanite idol worship, we see that God can take what the enemy means for evil and use it for good (Genesis 50:20). They end up serving the temple with its need for fuel for the sacrifices and water for cleansing. Instead of detracting from the worship of God, they assisted in it. Even generations later, at least one of them was among David's mighty men (1 Chronicles 12:4). His name meant Yahweh hears, which indicates the conversion of the Gibeonites to the God of Israel. The Ark of the Covenant was even hosted in Gibeon for a time (2 Chronicles 1:3). The Gibeonites were also part of rebuilding and fortifying Jerusalem so the worship of God could be done safely.

King Saul's zeal to cleanse Israel of Canaanites by forsaking the covenant Joshua made with them was as misplaced as making the covenant in the first place. In the New Testament we see that wonderful promise that God works all things together for good to those who love God

(Romans 8:28). He even takes our mistakes and the enemy's tactics and turns them around to help us. Sometimes it is growth through testing. At other times, like in this account, it is a blessing that we did not deserve or even see coming. What a wonderful and gracious God we serve! Everything is for His glory.

In the rebuilding of the walls of Jerusalem, ninety-five sons of Gibeon assisted. They no longer seem to be mere servants, but a part of the Israelite nation. Their association with the temple seems to have brought about a full conversion and inclusion into the nation.

Whether you relate to the Gibeonites or the leaders who failed to seek God's direction or perhaps the complaining people, the message here is that we serve an amazing God of grace and mercy. He is not willing that any should perish (2 Peter 3:9). Though the sins of the Gibeonites deserved death, God not only saw the heart of Rahab and her family, but that of the whole tribe of Gibeon and welcomed their conversion. This reminds me of a passage in Ephesians about us. *"As for you, you were dead in your trespasses and sins in which you used to live, when you followed the ways of this world, and of the ruler of the kingdom of the air, the spirit who is now at work in those who are disobedient. All of us also lived among them at one time, gratifying our sinful nature and following its desires and thoughts. Like the rest, we were by nature objects of wrath.* (Just like the entire Canaanite region.) *But because of his great love for us, God, who is rich in mercy made us alive with Christ even when we were dead in transgressions-- it is by grace you have been saved.* Ephesians 2:1-5 (NIV)

We were all Gibeonites - destined for destruction, but we heard of the mighty works of God. The fear of the LORD grew in our hearts, and we too became His servants. We serve a temple of living stones. The cornerstone of this glorious temple is Christ Jesus (Ephesians 2:20). Instead of sacrifices we present ourselves as living sacrifices, holy, acceptable to God, which is our reasonable act of worship (Romans 12:1).

Questions:
1 What lesson is being driven home?
2 What spiritual parallels have we seen so far?
3 What motivated the Gibeonites?
4 What was their method of deceit?
5 What verse declares Israel's big mistake?
6 What was Joshua supposed to do?
7 What parallel do we see in offering peace to a city?
8 How do we go about fighting the good fight of faith?
9 Why do we so often misjudge our situation?
10 How are we like Gibeonites?

Conquest Joshua 10:1-27

Israel had been taught, through several painful lessons, the need to listen to God. There was the initial loss at Ai followed by the Gibeonite deception. The consequences were long term, one of which they faced in our chapter for today. The leaders of Israel were to be commended for keeping their oath to be in alliance with Gibeon despite the protests of the people (Psalm 15:4). Now that commitment would be tested.

¹ As soon as Adoni-zedek, king of Jerusalem, heard how Joshua had captured Ai and had devoted it to destruction, doing to Ai and its king as he had done to Jericho and its king, and how the inhabitants of Gibeon had made peace with Israel and were among them, ² he feared greatly, because Gibeon was a great city, like one of the royal cities, and because it was greater than Ai, and all its men were warriors. Joshua 10:1-2 The king of

Jerusalem's name means Lord of Justice. It could also mean Leader of Retribution which is more fitting for what he is attempting to do. But he is about to meet the real Lord of Justice! He wanted to deal a crushing blow to Gibeon to warn the rest of his allies that they better not side with Israel as Gibeon had done. Gibeon's men were known to be warriors and their capitulation to Israel was a crushing blow to the region's alliances against Israel. Adoni-zedek greatly feared that he would be the next king to be hung in front of his city gates. Instead of following the example of the Gibeonites and recognizing that Israel's God was the God of gods, he turned to his allies.

³ So Adoni-zedek king of Jerusalem sent to Hoham king of Hebron, to Piram king of Jarmuth, to Japhia king of Lachish, and to Debir king of Eglon, saying, ⁴ "Come up to me and help me, and let us strike Gibeon. For it has made peace with Joshua and with the people of Israel." ⁵ Then the five kings of the Amorites, the king of Jerusalem, the king of Hebron, the king of Jarmuth, the king of Lachish, and the king of Eglon, gathered their forces and went up with all their armies and encamped against Gibeon and made war against it. Joshua 10:3-5 The kings of five cities of southern Israel gathered their armies and came against Gibeon. It is interesting to me that they were so well informed. They knew what had happened to Jericho and Ai, what had been done to their kings, how Gibeon made peace with Israel, and the name of Israel's leader, Joshua. Just as Jericho and Ai knew about Israel's deliverance from Egypt and the victories in the wilderness, Adoni-zedek probably knew about those victories too. Since we know that Rahab knew of those things, surely word had spread throughout the region.

⁶ And the men of Gibeon sent to Joshua at the camp in Gilgal, saying, "Do not relax your hand from your servants. Come up to us quickly and save us and help us, for all the kings of the Amorites who dwell in the hill country are gathered against us." Joshua 10:6 Gibeon sent word to Joshua about the united armies that gathered against them. This is what I call a Holy Spirit set up. Joshua would have eventually led a battle against those cities, perhaps one at a time. But Adoni-zedek's fear hastened their demise. His "good idea" of punishing Gibeon was going to be their undoing. Gibeon's plea was for Joshua to push on in his war on the region. *"Do not relax your hand..."* In other words, keep pressing forward and take the land, but of course that meant to defend their new ally first. Instead of being a warning to the allies of the region not to make an alliance with Israel, Israel defending Gibeon should have been an encouragement to surrender and live. But the hearts of the people in that region were so hardened they would not consider that option (Joshua 11:20). As we saw in the previous passage, they could have lived and had a future with Israel as the Gibeonites did.

⁷ So Joshua went up from Gilgal, he and all the people of war with him, and all the mighty men of valor. ⁸ And the LORD said to Joshua, "Do not fear them, for I have given them into your hands. Not a man of them shall stand before you." Joshua 10:7,8 When Joshua got the news, he immediately gathered his forces and began to move toward Gibeon. He had acted before without the Word of the Lord with disastrous results, so now he was listening for God's instruction. God had given these kings and their armies into Joshua's hands. *"Not a man of them shall stand before you"* means that no one could be successful against Israel. Again, the Word from the Lord sounds like a done deal, *"I have given them into your hands."* When the Word of God tells us that "greater is He who is in you than He who is in the world," we can be sure the same is true for us in a spiritual sense. In Jesus we are victorious (1 John 4:4).

⁹ So Joshua came upon them suddenly, having marched up all night from Gilgal. ¹⁰ And the LORD threw them into a panic before Israel, who struck them with a great blow at Gibeon and chased them by the way of the ascent of Beth-horon and struck them as far as Azekah and Makkedah. Joshua 10:9,10 Encouraged and emboldened by God's promise, the army of Israel marched all night and surprised the armies that had come against Gibeon. The LORD assisted in the battle by throwing those armies into a panic. Many died there and the rest fled as Israel's army pursued them.

Let us not forget that the Israelites had been slaves just forty years earlier. They were not trained in warfare and had only the alliance with Gibeon. They had conquered territory on the other side of the Jordan, and Joshua led the army before, but their victories were due to God keeping the promise He gave to Abraham (Genesis 17:8). The next verse shows us that, like the victory they experienced with Jericho, the battle belongs to the Lord (1 Samuel 17:47).

¹¹ And as they fled before Israel, while they were going down the ascent of Beth-horon, the LORD threw down large stones from heaven on them as far as Azekah, and they died. There were more who died because of the hailstones than the sons of Israel killed with the sword. Joshua 10:11 The fleeing armies went up over the ridge of Beth-horon and as they came down the other side the LORD caused large hailstones to rain down on them which killed more of them than were killed by Israel's swords. This is more evidence that the conquest of the land was God's judgment on their wickedness.

¹² At that time Joshua spoke to the LORD in the day when the LORD gave the Amorites over to the sons of

Israel, and he said in the sight of Israel, "Sun, stand still at Gibeon, and moon, in the Valley of Aijalon." 13 And the sun stood still, and the moon stopped, until the nation took vengeance on their enemies. Is this not written in the Book of Jashar? The sun stopped in the midst of heaven and did not hurry to set for about a whole day. Joshua 10:12,13 This is a favorite of atheists who want to disprove the Bible. Of course, they start with the presupposition that there is no all-powerful God, and that the Bible is completely literal and not written from the perspective of the viewer. In that sense they are more literalists than we are. We readily accept the fact that Joshua was speaking of the way things appear to him while we now know the earth is rotating around the sun. But critics would then say that the earth stopping its rotation would bring catastrophe to the planet, ocean tsunamis of unimaginable magnitude among other catastrophes. But that is because they don't believe God is over all things and miracles are possible.

There are five main interpretations in commentaries of what took place. The five main approaches are: the earth stopped rotating, the sun's light lingered, the sun's light was blocked, a special sign was involved, and lastly the passage is figurative. Howard's own position is to favor the figurative option, seeing the unique day's existence "not because of some extraordinary astronomical phenomenon but because the Lord listened to the voice of a man and fought for Israel." Alternative explanations abound, such as a solar eclipse on September 30, 1131 B.C. or the passage of the planet Mars within about 70,000 miles of earth around 1404 B.C., which is nearer the right date for Joshua.[xii]

The sun was about to go down. This tells me a couple of things. When we have heavy hail, the clouds are so dark you can't tell where the sun is. These huge hailstones were not a natural event. They were literally heaven sent. If the sun set, many of the fleeing warriors would have escaped in the darkness.

Joshua could see what was happening, so he shouted out for all to hear for the sun and moon to stand still. We would say for time to stop moving forward. We see that in some sci-fi movies. Everyone is frozen except for the ones who caused time to stop. I really can't imagine how it happened, but for about an extra twelve hours it seemed time stood still as Israel's army finished most of what was left of the armies that came against Gibeon. Apparently, at the time of the writing of the book of Joshua, there was a history book called the Book of Jashir that recorded the very long day.

[14] There has been no day like it before or since, when the LORD heeded the voice of a man, for the LORD fought for Israel. [15] So Joshua returned, and all Israel with him, to the camp at Gilgal. Joshua 10:14,15 What is so amazing is not that time seemed to stand still, but that God took orders from Joshua. Just so we don't go around ordering God to do things, the author says there was no day like it or since when the Lord heeded the voice of a man. There is a mistranslation of Isaiah 45:11 which in the KJV[xiii] says "command ye me." Newer translations look at the context and translate it "will you command me?" as if asking if anyone would be so impudent to give God orders. So, there are those folks who go around commanding God to do things. But when we look at the context of that verse, God is asking if we would be so arrogant as to command Him. And yet, Joshua, obviously led by the Holy Spirit and carrying out God's instruction did command God to extend the day until the enemy was almost entirely defeated.

In the New Testament we are told to ask, seek, and knock (Matthew 7:7), and to come confidently before the throne of grace to find help in time of need (Hebrews 4:16). But that is very different from commanding God.

138

We are also told that, *"If we ask anything according to His will, He hears us."* 1 John 5:14 That is what Joshua did. But the Scriptures also warn us that when we ask and do not receive it is because we are asking according to our passions (James 4:3). We can be confident in our prayers when we know we are praying God's will.

God intervened that His will might be done in the judgment on the Amorites. We call such supernatural intervention a miracle. In this case it was a miracle for the cause of judgment but also of providing the new home for the tribes of Israel.

I imagine that Gibeon was reassured that they had made the right choice in aligning with the God of Israel. If they had chosen to resist Israel, those hailstones would have been on their heads. Are you on the right side in this cosmic battle over the souls of men? Have you chosen the all-powerful and good God who loves you and does not want you to perish? When you join his side, it does not mean that you will not have battles. If you join his spiritual army you will have to fight the forces of darkness that would hinder you (Ephesians 6:11,12). But you can know you are on the winning side, and you will see Him act on your behalf in amazing ways.

Jesus is preparing a place for us too (John 14:1). That place is completely free of all evil, for the Bible predicts that the armies of this world will unite to try and stop Him (Revelation 19:19). But nothing can stop our God. That place is free of all evil, even the evil within us, and will be our home more so than any place you ever experienced in this life. The closest thing here is a group of believers who love Jesus and one another (John 13:35). If we want a greater experience of heaven to come, we need to be ruthless in dealing with that rebellion that remains in our own hearts.

[16] These five kings fled and hid themselves in the cave at Makkedah. [17] And it was told to Joshua, "The five kings have been found, hidden in the cave at Makkedah." [18] And Joshua said, "Roll large stones against the mouth of the cave and set men by it to guard them, [19] but do not stay there yourselves. Pursue your enemies; attack their rear guard. Do not let them enter their cities, for the LORD your God has given them into your hand." [20] When Joshua and the sons of Israel had finished striking them with a great blow until they were wiped out, and when the remnant that remained of them had entered into the fortified cities, [21] then all the people returned safe to Joshua in the camp at Makkedah. Not a man moved his tongue against any of the people of Israel. Joshua 10:16-21

The five kings hid in a cave but were found out. Joshua had large stones placed over the mouth of the cave and placed a guard there while the army continued to pursue the enemy. Joshua reminded the army that God had given them the victory, so they pursued the remnant of the coalition all the way to their cities. Some had escaped, but

140

with their forces diminished, the cities would be an easy conquest as the end of the chapter describes. Then they returned to their camp where the five kings were trapped.

²² Then Joshua said, "Open the mouth of the cave and bring those five kings out to me from the cave." ²³ And they did so, and brought those five kings out to him from the cave, the king of Jerusalem, the king of Hebron, the king of Jarmuth, the king of Lachish, and the king of Eglon. ²⁴ And when they brought those kings out to Joshua, Joshua summoned all the men of Israel and said to the chiefs of the men of war who had gone with him, "Come near; put your feet on the necks of these kings." Then they came near and put their feet on their necks. Joshua 10:22-24 Joshua had the kings taken out of the cave and lain on the ground before his army. Then he had the commanders put their feet on the necks of the kings. It was a sign of complete authority over them. In Scripture "putting under the feet" is a term used in those times to express complete authority. Jesus quoted Psalm 110 in which it is declared that God will put all His enemies under Jesus' feet (Psalm 110:1). The greatest enemy is death, which Jesus has already conquered for us (Revelation 1:18).

²⁵ And Joshua said to them, "Do not be afraid or dismayed; be strong and courageous. For thus the LORD will do to all your enemies against whom you fight." ²⁶ And afterward Joshua struck them and put them to death, and he hanged them on five trees. And they hung on the trees until evening. ²⁷ But at the time of the going down of the sun, Joshua commanded, and they took them down from the trees and threw them into the cave where they had hidden themselves, and they set large stones against the mouth of the cave, which remain to this very day. Joshua 10:22-27 Then Joshua commanded the people what God had commanded of him. *"Do not be afraid or dismayed; be strong and courageous!"* He declared that the LORD

would do the same with all the enemies they fought. They had yet to take on the northern alliance. Then the kings were executed by Joshua. Their dead bodies were then displayed hanging from a tree (Deuteronomy 21:22,23), and that evening buried in the cave in which they hid.

Most of us are in a similar position to Israel in this passage. We have faced trials in our lives and fight spiritual battles. We are standing in victory because the Lord fights for us. But we need to be strong and courageous for the battles that lie ahead. The enemy of our soul will do all he can to make us ineffective, discouraged, and fearful. Never forget that the battle belongs to the Lord! We look to our Commander, follow His directions, arm ourselves with the sword of the Spirit (Ephesians 6:17), and persevere until He brings us to the home He has prepared for us.

In Revelation it is predicted that people will try to hide from the wrath of God in dens and caves of the earth (Revelation 6:15,16), but there is no hiding from God (Hebrews 4:13). The first couple that sinned hid in the garden (Genesis 3:8). But instead of the wrath they deserved, they were shown great grace, even given coverings for their nakedness (Genesis 3:21). They had another chance recognize the Word of the Lord is given for their good. We are all recipients of those numerous chances, but those who end up hardening their hearts toward the goodness of God will find their hiding place is discovered, and they must face the real Lord of Justice. Though He is not willing that any should perish (2 Peter 3:9), He will not force us to accept His grace. And should we refuse His grace, we will have to receive His justice. Either we accept that He took the justice we deserve, or we will have to receive it ourselves. God will always be just, and we wouldn't want it any other way (Psalm 36:6).

Questions:
1 What lesson had been driven home?
2 What is ironic about the king of Jerusalem's name?
3 Why did he gather a coalition against Gibeon?
4 Why didn't they surrender to Israel?
5 How did God assist in the battle?
6 Do miracles really happen?
7 Are we to command God?
8 Why could Joshua do so?
9 How can we get a taste of what is to come?
10 Why do we need to be strong and courageous?

Taking Our Land Joshua 10:28 – 13:1

At this point in the book of Joshua we have long lists of battles and the boundaries of the different tribes. We are not going to read over it all. Many of the place names are unknown to us today. I am going to hit some of the highlights and the overarching principle which is that God is faithful to keep His promises, but we need to cooperate with Him to receive the fullness of the blessings He wants to give us. When we don't, we end up suffering the consequences of our lack of submission to Jesus.

The campaign to defeat the cities of the Negev in chapter 10 verses 29 to 43 probably took months. We have a brief summary in those verses. Town after town fell to Israel's forces and were devoted to destruction. Israel was successful because, as is declared in verse 42, the LORD God fought for Israel.

The justice of God is something that the fallen nature of man does not like to consider. Can God decide when a person or nation has come to a place where they will never return from rebellion against all that is good? He does every day. He has numbered our days (Job 14:4). Each of us continues to live because either we have not grown so hardened, or we are still growing in grace to prepare ourselves for eternity in His presence. We cannot say when it is the right time for a person to die. Perhaps God spares people by taking them before they make wrong decisions. We must leave that to God and trust He knows each of our hearts better than we know our own.

But there will come a day when our world, like that of the Amorites, will find their iniquity reaches God's limit (Genesis 15:16). There will be a day when the army of heaven does to the whole world what Joshua did to the Negev (Revelation 19:15). Thankfully, there will be an end to evil and rebellion against God. But that will only come after those who survive those days live under the perfect reign of Christ on earth and then are willingly deceived for the last time to follow Lucifer in an attack upon God.

We would like to think, as many religions and cults do, that someday everyone will receive the love of God. That is what God desires, but the prophets, including Jesus, say it just won't happen (Mark 9:43). They predict a final battle when the entire world will unite to fight against the return of Christ (Revelation 16:14). The vast majority of the world will have sworn allegiance to the antichrist who promises peace and prosperity but also demands that the world worship him. He will make war on those who worship Jesus and try to annihilate them (Revelation 13:7,8; Daniel 7:21). The heart of man is desperately evil (Jeremiah 17:9), and the antichrist will certainly stroke the egos of all who will join him. He will present himself as the answer to all our problems, a superhero.

A false prophet will cause people to worship the antichrist and will even show miraculous signs (Revelation 13:13,14). People will not be deceived because he is so clever, but rather because he will tell them what they want to hear (2 Timothy 4:3). He will claim that no repentance is needed, nothing will be called sinful, except to oppose him. He will tell the world they should do as they wish and forget all the taboos of ancient religions. Jesus said it will be like the days of Noah (Matthew 24:37). At that time, the thoughts of men's hearts were only evil continually (Genesis 6:5). He compared those coming days to the days of Lot (Luke 17:28). The men of the city were so lustful that even when struck with blindness the tried to commit vile acts. The destruction by the flood, the brimstone from heaven upon Sodom, as well as this section of Joshua all foreshadow that coming judgment on the entire world (Ecclesiastes 1:9).

We all wish that everyone would see the destructiveness of trying to be our own god, but we cannot make people see what they refuse to see. Jesus came to set the captives free, but many prefer enslavement to their passions. We can be sure God will give us every chance to turn from lies to the truth, from darkness to light (Ezekiel 33:11). But some will never accept any lord but self. Some people even proudly declare that if God would condemn people to hell, they don't want Him as their God.

Just as Rahab and Gibeon chose to ally themselves with the God of Israel, so we too have that choice. Every city in Canaan had that choice. Even after hearing of all the mighty things God had done for Israel, they chose to fight against Israel's God. So will it be at the end of this age. Thank God that we have bowed to the King who loves us and gave Himself for us. His grace helped us open our eyes. By His grace we chose Him and now we are growing increasingly into His likeness (2 Corinthians 3:18).

This section of Joshua was a physical battle, but it had deep spiritual roots. God's command through Moses was to tear down their places of worship and their idols (Deuteronomy 7:3-5; 12:2,3). God knew Israel would not finish the job, and so He added the command not to intermarry with them lest they cause Israel to worship their gods. If they disobeyed, Israel would become idolatrous and deserve the same fate. At different stages in the nation's history many did so, and the nation eventually did go into captivity just as Moses predicted.

You can fight against God, or you can surrender to His goodness and experience His grace. It is a matter of where your allegiance lies in this spiritual battle over the souls of mankind.

Because our old nature never truly leaves us while we are in this life, we will often try to blend both worlds. We are great at justifying or reasoning things to be other than what Scripture declares them to be. We choose beliefs that let us do as we please apart from God and then add some worship, a little Bible study, and some prayer with those beliefs. That is just like Israel's later years when they came to the temple and made their sacrifices while blatantly disobeying what God instructed them to do (Malachi 1:7). They will make offerings to other gods right in sight of the temple. But God is described as a jealous God (Exodus 20:5). He is not jealous like mankind is for selfish reasons, but instead He is jealous for our good and for truth. When we blend the old nature and other religions with what Jesus has done for us, He will discipline us as He did Israel.

When the southern coalition was defeated, the kings of the north joined forces to try to resist Israel. God again encouraged Joshua: *6 And the LORD said to Joshua, "Do not be afraid of them, for tomorrow at this time I will give over all of them, slain, to Israel. You shall hamstring their horses and burn their chariots with fire." 7 So Joshua and all his warriors came suddenly against them by the waters of Merom and fell upon them. 8 And the LORD gave them into the hand of Israel,* Joshua 11:6-8a "Do not be afraid!" This huge coalition of forces with superior weaponry is coming against you but there is no need to fear. God and one are a majority! The Lord gave the victory, and He will give us the victory in the spiritual realm as well (Psalm 60:12).

When the antichrist is killing Christians, we will not need to fear. That is because our Joshua will be victorious in the end. Jesus commanded us not to fear those who kill the body but have no more that they can do. He said that we should fear the One who can destroy soul and body in hell (Matthew 10:28). If we fear anything, it should be fearing that our weaknesses will turn us against Jesus by compromising the truth, and then be judged for that rebellion. But we have a promise that Jesus will finish what He started in us (Philippians 1:6). We know He is a good Shepherd and does not lose His sheep (John 18:9). But make every effort to not wander off and be in need of discipline.

I asked in previous sermons why the people of the land would fight a force whose God could drop giant walls flat and stop a river at flood stage. Why would they resist when hailstones from heaven killed more of their enemies than swords did? The answer is in verse 20. *20 For it was the LORD's doing to harden their hearts that they should come against Israel in battle, in order that they should be devoted to destruction and should receive no mercy but be destroyed, just as the LORD commanded Moses.* Joshua 11:20 God hardened their hearts. It was the same with Pharaoh. The account of Pharaoh's resistance against God gives us a clue as to what was happening in Canaan. Pharaoh hardened his own heart numerous times before God hardened it.

Man can yield without surrendering. In essence, that is what Pharaoh did. He let the people go but then went after them with his army. If the nations, other than the Gibeonites had surrendered and become slaves, Israelites would soon be worshiping their idols. God hardened the enemy's hearts because He knew they would not change. I believe He does the same today. I witness debates where the liberal humanist is defeated at every turn but still walks away pridefully thinking he won. When a person is beyond the point of no return and determined to rebel, God will harden their heart to their own destruction.

23 So Joshua took the whole land, according to all that the LORD had spoken to Moses. And Joshua gave it for an inheritance to Israel according to their tribal allotments. And the land had rest from war. Joshua 11:23 Because Scripture tells us that all these things happened as examples for us (1 Corinthians 10:6), let us consider the spiritual application. We also have the promises of God and a divine inheritance (2 Peter 1:4; 1 Peter 1:4). And we have a great enemy who would like to keep us from taking the land. He, like the Canaanites, is under the wrath of God, devoted to destruction. Like them, his heart is hardened to a point of no return. He knows he will lose for he has seen the mighty hand of God, and yet he attacks us with his legions.

However, we have been promised to be victorious, for the same power that worked for Israel is working for us. The LORD will give us the victory. That doesn't mean that we won't have battles or suffer. Considering the age of Caleb, we can estimate these battles took seven years. Unlike the battle with the southern kings, God did not send hail to assist in the battle. It was up to the men of Israel using their swords.

We use the sword of the Spirit, the Word of God, to fight our battles, just as our commander Jesus did when tempted in the wilderness (Ephesians 6:17; Matthew 4:4).

We too are told not to fear, for Jesus, our Joshua, has already given the enemy into our hands, for greater is He who is in you than He who is in the world (1 John 4:4). *19Behold, I have given you authority to tread on serpents and scorpions, and over all the power of the enemy, and nothing shall hurt you. [20] Nevertheless, do not rejoice in this, that the spirits are subject to you, but rejoice that your names are written in heaven."* (Luke 10:19,20).

We show no mercy to the influence of the world, to our old nature, and the devil. Those influences are to be given no quarter in our lives. If we cling to the things devoted to destruction, then like Achan, we put ourselves under their curse. But if we fight on until our hearts are cleared of all the idolatrous influences, we too will have rest from war. Our Joshua, Jesus, will give us our inheritance, heavenly homes we did not build, but that He has prepared for us (Joshua 24:13; John 14:2).

Chapter 12 gives a list of all the lands the Israelites conquered on both sides of the Jordan River. Joshua did all that the LORD commanded through Moses. He is a foreshadow of Jesus who did all that the Father commanded Him. However, some of the tribes did not finish the work assigned to them. God predicted this through Moses and warned them not to intermarry or worship their idols (Deuteronomy 7:3,4).

We can have our own list of victories. Our battle is not seven years, but since seven represents completeness, we are to see it as our whole life. The victories we rack up are over our old nature and helping others be victorious. It would be a good exercise to journal victories the LORD gives you. Let me give you examples: 7/1/19 - victory over the temptation to lust when the king of sexual fantasy was put to death at Slide Rock State Park. 12/12/20 - victory over greed when I obeyed the Spirit and gave that money to John to help with his rent. There the king of greed was executed in Cottonwood. 3/1/21 victory over selfishness about time when I gave the day to help Jim with the work on his house. There I slew the king of "My free time!" You get the idea.

Through verse six we have a list of every victory on the east side of the Jordan while Moses was still living. From verse seven to the end of the chapter the list of the kings Joshua conquered is covered. That concludes the first half of the book.

Chapter 13-21 is the second half, the distribution of the land to the tribes. Chapter 13 focuses on the land given to half the tribe of Manasseh, Gad, and Reuben. The chapter begins with the need to divide the land before Joshua dies for the people respect Joshua's instruction. There was no great leader to follow Joshua, so the tribes could have ended up fighting over the land if it was not divided while Joshua lived.

We are told that the entire land had not yet been conquered. The people that were left will cause most of the problems Israel experiences in the future. One group is the Philistines who live along the coast. They were probably from Crete originally and settled that region by driving the Avvim to the south.

When we come to Christ, we have some mighty victories that start our new life. We have realized our need for forgiveness, our fallen nature, and surrendered our lives to follow our captain. We often begin by giving up some of the obvious things that held us captive. It may take some time, but with God's help we prevail. But then we read in Scripture that there is more to conquer. *"This is the land that yet remains."* We find that we have been given an inheritance, and just like these Israelites, we must go out and take it, knowing that God goes before us.

They had the description of their land like a title deed. We have the description of our land described in the promises of the New Testament. It is a covenant that first guarantees eternal life (John 3:36). It doesn't just mean living forever. It means being in a right relationship with God and communing with Him forever. That is the land in general, but we each have our specific part. The land that remains to be taken is our calling and gifts within our life/land.

But let us first look at claiming that land of a right relationship and communion with God, for this is where we all begin. Remember that what they first did was to circumcise the males. All who had not been circumcised in the desert entered into that covenant. It pictures a heart that is tender toward God, a heart that readily receives conviction. This was the sign, an outer sign, like baptism is today. We will have some creek baptisms after church on Easter. Baptism declares we have joined ourselves with those who follow Jesus. It makes us vulnerable like it made them vulnerable. An outward declaration that we have died with Christ and been raised with Him means others will watch to see if it is real. They may mock us, unfriend us, and in some places expel us. In the early church it sometimes meant imprisonment or execution. So, the first step is a new identity. It should be obvious to others that we follow Christ as He becomes our first love. In some regions Christians even take on a new name.

Then there was the first big conquest. Jericho was impenetrable, as are some of our besetting sins, the habitual ones we are convicted to leave behind. The battle seems insurmountable, but Jesus is the victory in us. We shout the victory and watch the walls fall flat. Then it is up to us to destroy any remnant that would connect us to that vanquished sin. We dare not hide any small piece of in our hearts or it will destroy us.

Then in this honeymoon period where we feel so victorious, we face a little town of Ai, a problem we don't think is so big, and we go about trying to put it away. But we find it badly defeats us. We forgot to look to the Lord. We begin learning the lesson that we need to pray and seek God's direction from the Bible and the Spirit. The lesson is reinforced when we found we made a compromise we thought was insignificant but turned out to be with us for the rest of our life. That was pictured in the Gibeonite deception.

There are other major areas ahead that we can see in the battles with the northern kings. These can be major areas of our life, such as marriage and our occupation. How do we follow Christ in those areas where so many are defeated? Just like we did with Jericho and Ai, we get God's battle plans.

But now we have come to taking our inheritance in the land, or we could say in the body of Christ. This is what half the book deals with (1 Corinthians 12:7). The lot is cast into the lap, but the Lord determines the outcome (Proverbs 16:33). He assigns your place, your gifts, and your calling. And some of these areas that have yet to be taken still have giants to conquer. What church is God leading me to be a part of? What is my part in it? What classes or groups do I attend? How can I help make the church all God means it to be? Where is the need? How do I reach out to others who need to know Jesus' love and forgiveness? And as we begin to search our hearts and observe what God puts before us, with the Spirit's guidance we start to discern our land that is to be taken. That doesn't mean on Sunday only but every day and wherever we happen to be (Colossians 3.17).

This final claiming of the land allotted to us is being a vital member of the body of Christ, walking in the Spirit and the calling of God on our life (Galatians 5:25). That is when we find that even in all the activity there is rest in our souls. We are doing what God created us to do. We are enjoying fellowship with God and our brothers and sisters in Christ. We are laying up treasures in heaven, teaching disciples how to follow Jesus, and enjoying doing it (Matthew 28:19,20). Oh, it is work, but it is Christ empowered work. The outcome of our faith will be seen in our lives and the lives of those we influence. We are as close to home as you can experience in this life.

Dear brother and sister in Christ, how much of your promised land yet remains to be taken? What is your calling? Jericho and Ai may have been conquered, but there are still battles to fight. Have you found your place of service to the body? Are you marching forward in faith at our Captain's commands?

Questions:
1 Who is the only one who knows when it is the right time to die?
2 Will the world as we know it have a happy ending for all?
3 What does the Bible say about the fate of most people in the end?
4 Why would the antichrist want to kill Christians?
5 Why didn't the northern kings surrender?
6 Why would God harden their hearts?
7 Why would God do such a thing?
8 What land was yet to be taken?
9 What is the application to our own lives?
10 Have you discovered your calling?

Our Inheritance Joshua 13-15

God had fulfilled the 400-year- old promise to give the land in which Abraham had wandered to his descendants. They had miraculously been delivered from slavery in Egypt by the miracle of the plagues, been sustained in the wilderness for forty years (Nehemiah 9:21), and conquered the tribes on both sides of the Jordan River. They had witnessed the hand of God in the stopping of the Jordan River at flood stage (Joshua 3:16), the walls of Jericho falling flat, and the hailstones rained down on the evil Amorites (Joshua 10:11). They knew God was in their midst and had chosen them as a people group (Deuteronomy 7:7,8).

I don't think they understood the extent of the promises God had given to Abraham. He had promised that he would be the father of many nations, not just Israel (Genesis 17:5). He had also promised his offspring would bless the world (Genesis 12:3). The Apostle Paul explains in the chapter the men's group recently studied, Romans chapter four, that God meant more than physical descendants or those who keep God's laws, but rather the people that follow in Abraham's footsteps of faith, believing and trusting in God (Romans 4:16,17). They are the nations of which Abraham is the father. They are the heirs of the promise, for we have been blessed in *the* descendant of Abraham, Jesus the Christ.

As they moved into the land promised to them, I believe their focus was on the fulfillment of receiving the land. Today we can see the fulfillment of the promise to bless the world in the contributions the Jewish people have made. Israelis have won more Nobel prizes per capita than the USA, Germany and France. Their medicines and current research are groundbreaking. Our former elder Gary Alden sent me some good news about Israeli research. The University of Tel Aviv is developing a nasal vaccine that will protect people from Alzheimer's and stroke. Bar Ilan University is studying a new drug that fights viruses by blood. It is called the Vecoy Trap because it tricks a virus into self-destruction. It will be very useful to fight Hepatitis, and in the future AIDS and Ebola. The Ichlov Center (Tel Aviv) has isolated a protein that makes colonoscopy unnecessary to detect colon cancer with a simple blood test. I could go on and on.

Even more importantly they received and preserved what we call the Old Testament upon which the legal system of the Western world was based (Romans 3:1,2). God blessed the world through this nation, but God's promise to Abraham was much broader. He is the father of not one nation, but many spiritual nations who believe by faith in what God has done for us in Jesus.

The physical descendants were about to divide the land among their tribes with the exception of the Levites. *[14] To the tribe of Levi alone Moses gave no inheritance. The offerings by fire to the LORD God of Israel are their inheritance, as he said to him.* Joshua 13:14 *[33] But to the tribe of Levi Moses gave no inheritance; the LORD God of Israel is their inheritance, just as he said to them.* Joshua 13:33 The Levites did not receive an area because they received the offerings by fire to support them. Leviticus describes which offerings and what portion of the offering was theirs. It was to be their provision. But much more frequently stated in the books of Moses is that the LORD is their inheritance. The privilege of serving the LORD in the sanctuary was to be more valuable to them than land. This foreshadows the New Testament saints. We have no inheritance in the world, but the LORD is our inheritance. We are satisfied and supplied by serving Him.

Joshua 14:3,4 tells us that they were given cities throughout Israel with pastureland for their flocks and herds. Numbers 19:20-32 instructs Israel that a tithe of all tithes goes to the priests. We can glean from other passages that the Levite clans took turns of service at certain times of the year. The clan for special service on feast days was chosen by lot. When it was a certain family's time to serve, the men would leave their wives and children to care for their herds and go to the temple. Even the men assigned for special tasks were chosen by lot. We have an example of this in Zechariah, the father of John the Baptist, serving in the Holy Place when the angel appeared to him (Luke 1:8,9).

God wanted the whole nation of Israel to be priests representing Him to the world (Exodus 19:6). They failed to fulfill that role, so now the task is for the people of faith who believe as Abraham did (2 Corinthians 2:14).

Following the shadow presented in the Levite priests of Israel, we see it is not wrong for us to own property, but we just don't see it as our main inheritance. It is merely a place for us to reside while we await our call to duty. Nor do we all minister fulltime. We are given opportunities now and then and that is our delight. To be chosen to serve and help others get to know our God is our inheritance. That is what we value. And there are times when we are chosen for a very special assignment, such as leading a person to salvation, or sharing the Word of God, or standing up for Biblical truth in this fallen world. The Lord Himself is our inheritance and that is one reason the New Testament calls all believers priests (1 Peter 2:5). That is one reason we are children of Abraham, for the Scripture says the LORD was his very great reward (Genesis 15:1).

We have come to the distribution of the land to the tribes that will be on the west side of the Jordan. *¹ These are the inheritances that the people of Israel received in the land of Canaan, which Eleazar the priest and Joshua the son of Nun and the heads of the fathers' houses of the tribes of the people of Israel gave them to inherit. ² Their inheritance was by lot, just as the LORD had commanded by the hand of Moses for the nine and one-half tribes.* Joshua 14:1,2 Moses had commanded that the sections of land be determined by lot. That left everything up to God so the distribution would be without prejudice. No one could complain, for it would be determined by the Lord. The author is careful to point out that Joshua does everything just as Moses commanded. He is faithful to the recorded Word of the Lord from Moses (Numbers 34:13).

But there was a promised exception to the division of land by lot. *⁶ Then the people of Judah came to Joshua at Gilgal. And Caleb the son of Jephunneh the Kenizzite said to him, "You know what the LORD said to Moses the man of God in Kadesh-barnea concerning you and me. ⁷ I was forty years old when Moses the servant of the LORD sent me from Kadesh-barnea to spy out the land, and I brought him word again as it was in my heart. ⁸ But my brothers who went up with me made the heart of the people melt; yet I wholly followed the LORD my God. ⁹ And Moses swore on that day, saying, 'Surely the land on which your foot has trodden shall be an inheritance for you and your children forever, because you have wholly followed the LORD my God.'* Joshua 14:6-9

Caleb and Joshua had been given a promise because of their faithfulness when they spied out the land (Deuteronomy 1:36). The hearts of the other ten spies melted with fear at the sight of the Anakim, an extremely tall race of people, and they convinced the people of Israel that there was no hope in taking the land (Numbers 13:31-33). Joshua and Caleb, however, wholly followed the LORD. They believed God's promises. They tried to convince the people that the protection of the enemy was removed and that the LORD would give them victory. The people responded by picking up stones to stone them (Numbers 14:10). Because of Joshua and Caleb's faithfulness, the LORD told Moses to tell them that they could choose any part of the land they wanted. The people were judged with forty years in the wilderness while the older generation died out. Only Joshua and Caleb would live to see the Promised Land. What a warning to not doubt the promises of God, and what an encouragement to have faith and believe (2 Chronicles 20:20)!

Caleb was forty years old when he first spied out the land. They were in the wilderness for another forty years, and then at least five years of warfare taking the Promised Land. Now at 85 years of age, Caleb could declare his strength was equal to that when he was 40. He chose the territory of the Anakim, the Goliath clan, the hill country with their great fortified cities. He said that the LORD *may* help him drive them out. He isn't cocky about it, but he knows God has promised to do it. He is sober minded. Unlike the older generation whose eyes were on the giants, Caleb's eyes were on the LORD. And with God's help he did get the job done, as we will see in the next chapter.

Three times in this chapter we read that Caleb wholly followed the LORD his God (verses 8, 9, 14). God said he had a different spirit (Numbers 14:24). That is a spirit that trusted the LORD and not the arm of the flesh.

In the Hebrew that (wholly following) *is quite a striking word—more striking than in the English. It is a pictorial word in the Hebrew, and describes a ship going out at full sail. Why, that is the very keynote of Caleb from beginning to end. He was the man he was, from the beginning to the end, because he was out and out— because there were no limitations and provisions with him... He "went in" for God and His cause, like a ship in full sail. He flung every power of body, and soul, and spirit like a free sheet to the winds of God's grace, and God's Spirit, and God's Providence. He "let go."[xv]*

This zealous dedication is so meaningful to me that I asked that my grandson be named Caleb. Caleb means dog in Hebrew, but it implies faithfulness, and that is one thing God desires from us because He is always faithful to us (1 Corinthians 4:2). Here is an 85-year-old man who when given the choice of the best of the land took the hardest to obtain but most treasured piece of real estate. He says he is as tough as he ever was, and he will do what others are afraid to do. He wholly followed the LORD his God and drove out the Anakim. So much for retirement. There is no retirement from serving the Lord as long as there is strength in our bones, nor do we retire from spiritual battles while we have breath. When we quit fighting, we lose, because the enemy never retires.

What stops us from being like Caleb and wholly following the LORD? When we consider what He has done for us, we realize He deserves nothing less. He reminds me of the Apostle Paul who declared, *"I have been crucified with Christ. It is no longer I who live but Christ who lives in me. The life that I now live in the flesh I live by the faith of the Son of God who loved me and gave Himself for me"* (Galatians 2:20).

The priests of Israel were commanded in the Laws of Moses to pass on their duties to younger people when they reached the age of fifty (Numbers 4:3). But that doesn't mean they retire. They just get a different assignment so others could experience serving in the temple.

Chapter 13 started the section of dividing the land because Joshua was no longer physically capable of continuing his role (Joshua 13:1). But Caleb was still physically fit and saw that God was with him. Caleb declared, *10 And now, behold, the LORD has kept me alive, just as he said, these forty-five years since the time that the LORD spoke this word to Moses, while Israel walked in the wilderness. And now, behold, I am this day eighty-five years old. 11 I am still as strong today as I was in the day that Moses sent me; my strength now is as my strength was then, for war and for going and coming.* Joshua 14:10,11 There was a job that others feared to do. He had the same faith now that he did 40 years earlier when he told the people in Numbers 13:30. *30 But Caleb quieted the people before Moses and said, "Let us go up at once and occupy it, for we are well able to overcome it."* He still had that fighting spirit of faith in God's power and faithfulness.

Spiritual vision means being able to see a situation from God's perspective, based on his self-revelation, and so to be able to go forward into that situation confident that God's purposes will indeed be fulfilled, trusting him and expecting him to work.[xvi]

Caleb continued, *12 So now give me this hill country of which the LORD spoke on that day, for you heard on that day how the Anakim were there, with great fortified cities. It may be that the LORD will be with me, and I shall drive them out just as the LORD said." 13 Then Joshua blessed him, and he gave Hebron to Caleb the son of Jephunneh for an inheritance. 14 Therefore Hebron became the inheritance of Caleb the son of Jephunneh the Kenizzite to this day, because he wholly followed the LORD, the God of Israel.* Joshua 14:12-14

Caleb could see what God desired. e claimed it because he knew it was God's will for him, for he wholly followed the LORD. He would prove to the nation that what he said 40 years earlier was still true, God is able to drive them out. That is real vision. In our time leaders are encouraged to cast a vision, but too often it is what they desire to see happen. It is their personal hope and dream. Caleb's vision was based on his relationship with the LORD. He inspired faith in the faithfulness of God.

How we need men like Caleb today, men who with hearts after God, not looking to what is in it for them, but how they might be of service to the King they love and bring Him glory! As God would sovereignly ordain it, my devotional passage in My Utmost for His Highest expressed this very idea so well, that I want to share it in full.

It was based on Mark 10:28 KJV *Then Peter began to say unto Him, Lo, we have left all, and have followed Thee.....Our Lord replies, in effect, that abandonment is for Himself, and not for what the disciples themselves will get from it. Beware of an abandonment which has the commercial spirit in it—'I am going to give myself to God because I want to be delivered from sin, because I want to be made holy.' All that is the result of being right with God, but that spirit is not of the essential nature of Christianity. Abandonment is not for anything at all. We have got so commercialized that we only go to God for something from Him, and not for Himself. It is like saying—'No, Lord, I don't want Thee, I want myself; but I want myself clean and filled with the Holy Ghost; I want to be put in Thy showroom and be able to say—"This is what God has done for me." 'If we only give up something to God because we want more back, there is nothing of the Holy Spirit in our abandonment; it is miserable commercial self-interest. That we gain heaven, that we are delivered from sin, that we are made useful to God—these things never enter as considerations into real abandonment, which is a personal sovereign preference for Jesus Christ Himself.*

When we come up against the barriers of natural relationship, where is Jesus Christ? Most of us desert Him—'Yes, Lord, I did hear Thy call; but my mother is in the road, my wife, my self-interest, and I can go no further.' 'Then,' Jesus says, 'you cannot be My disciple.' The test of abandonment is always over the neck of natural devotion. Go over it, and God's own abandonment will embrace all those you had to hurt in abandoning. Beware of stopping short of abandonment to God. Most of us know abandonment in vision only.[xvii]

Caleb was abandoned to God. He could have picked a nice pastureland that had already been taken with a stream and city with walls already built and ready to be occupied. But he knew that wasn't God's will. He had a heart to do whatever God wanted, no matter how difficult. He had a heart that matched his name, faithful. And when he sensed God wanted him to take the hardest area yet to be taken, he didn't give his age as an excuse, but instead saw his physical strength remained for that purpose to which God had called him.

13 According to the commandment of the LORD to Joshua, he gave to Caleb the son of Jephunneh a portion among the people of Judah, Kiriath-arba, that is, Hebron (Arba was the father of Anak). 14 And Caleb drove out from there the three sons of Anak, Sheshai and Ahiman and Talmai, the descendants of Anak. Joshua 15:13-14 Hebron was special because it had the cave where the patriarchs were buried. Caleb conquered giants because God was with him. He did it because he knew God is faithful. He did it because he wholly followed the Lord and had a different spirit. What was true for the Levites was true for Caleb, the Lord was his reward. Is He your reward? There is nothing greater! Anything else falls way short and will never satisfy in the end. Nothing else is worthy of our faithful devotion (Revelation 5:12). If there is something else in your life that you are following, I humbly ask you to reconsider. The LORD says to those who follow wholly after Him what He said to Abraham, "I am your shield, your very great reward!" Genesis 15:3

Questions:
1 Why can we say we are heirs of the promise to Abraham?
2 How have the Jews blessed the world?
3 What did the Levites inherit?
4 Why is our inheritance the same?
5 Why was the land divided by lots?

6 Why were Caleb and Joshua exceptions?
7 Why didn't the Israelites enter the first time?
8 How was Caleb different from other people?
9 How can abandonment to God be *miserable commercial self-interest?*
10 What did Caleb choose and why?
11 Who or what have you chosen to follow? Why?

Pass It On Joshua 20-22

We are skipping over chapters 16 through 19 that deal with the distribution of the conquered land to the various tribes. There are a several noteworthy passages that can be lessons for us today. One passage presents an interesting account of the tribe of Manasseh complaining that the land they received was not enough because they were so numerous, and they could not drive out the people there who had iron chariots. It was some of the most fertile land in the nation. Joshua told them because their tribe was so numerous, they should get to it and drive those people out and clear the forest for farming. Don't complain, get to work (17:16-18). Remember that the areas were distributed by lot. That meant that the land they received was God's choice not Joshua's.

We can learn from this that God assigns us our lot in life. We tend to wish for something different, as the grass always looks greener on the other side. We end up complaining to God. But remember, He has assigned us our lot in life for a reason. Sometimes it is to stretch our faith. Instead of complaining, we should give thanks, stretch our faith muscles, get to work, and see what God will do through us in the situation He has allowed (Romans 5:3-5).

In chapter 20 the cities of refuge were assigned. Even as we near the end of the book of Joshua, we find it recorded that Joshua was faithful to do all that the LORD spoke through Moses. Moses instructed that cities of refuge were to be appointed throughout Israel as places of safety for anyone, Israelite or foreigner, who accidentally killed a person. The example of an ax head flying off the handle and causing a death is given in Deuteronomy 19:5. The family of the one who died would be seeking revenge, a life for a life (Exodus 21:23). These cities appointed in every area of the land would protect the person who took a life until a trial proved him innocent or guilty. If it was shown that he hated the person before that man died, he would not be sheltered. This implies what we would call premeditation. If guilty, he would be put out of the city. If innocent, he could stay protected until the death of the current high priest.

Until the death of the high priest foreshadows Jesus our great high priest whose death atones for our guilt and makes us innocent (Hebrews 4:14). Perhaps the randomness of the time one would have to stay in the city would by God's sovereign design be punishment for the degree of negligence of the manslayer. He would be separated from his family and property, but his life was spared.

A missionary to a remote tribe in Indonesia found the tribe had a similar practice. Instead of a city it was a circle of stones. The missionary used the cultural practice to explain that Jesus is our place of refuge. If we are found in Him, the destroyer is not allowed to take our life. This was the breakthrough they needed to convey the message of salvation in Christ to that tribe. Jesus is our city of refuge. He declares us innocent because His death paid our sin debt. The Avenger, Satan, cannot execute judgment on us if we stay in Jesus.

The cities of refuge were scattered in such a way that they would not be far from wherever you lived in

Israel. In the same way, the Word of God tells us that Jesus is near to us wherever we are (Romans 10:8; Acts 17:27; Psalm 139:7-10), just as the tabernacle was in the middle of the camp, as close as possible to each tribe. While we have not committed a murder, intentional or unintentional, we are guilty and condemned, for the Scripture declares that the soul that sins must die (Ezekiel 18:4). Sin is treason against God, and we are all sinners (Romans 3:23,24). He has every right to condemn us to hell. But unlike the cities of refuge, even though we are guilty, in His mercy He became a place of refuge where we might run to escape the justice we deserve. Jesus, our refuge, took that punishment upon Himself on the cross which satisfied the justice of God. Run to Him and find life everlasting freedom and from condemnation (Romans 8:1; John 10:28). No wonder the psalmist wrote, *22 The LORD redeems the life of his servants; none of those who take refuge in him will be condemned.* Psalm 34:22

Josephus tells us that where the road to a city of refuge came to an intersection, the way to the city of refuge had to remain clearly marked. The way to our refuge in Jesus is clearly marked as well, for the Scriptures tell us in numerous verses to believe on the Lord Jesus Christ and we will be saved (Acts 16:31). We can be that signpost when we see a desperate soul fleeing for safety by pointing the way to Jesus.

A magazine called Christian Age suggested that we too have six cities of refuge:

I. Our first city of refuge is prayer. Whatever trouble comes to us, we can run to prayer for help, as the man of old ran to the city of refuge.

II. Our second city of refuge is the Bible. When Jesus was tempted three times by the devil in the wilderness to do wrong, every time His heart ran to the

Bible as a city of refuge and quoted some precious promise.

III. A third city of refuge is sacred song. If our hearts and voices are full of sweet and pure songs about God, and heaven, and doing good, they will keep away a great many wicked thoughts and evil words.

IV. The fourth city of refuge is trust in God as our Father. A child was asked the question, "What is faith?" She answered," God has spoken, and I believe it." That is a part of what it means to trust in God.

V. Our fifth city of refuge is the Holy Spirit as our Guide.

VI. The sixth city of refuge, the last one and the most precious, is Jesus as our Saviour.[xviii] Of course all of them together point to Jesus!

Once the Levites had been assigned their cities of refuge, all the land had been allotted. Then we read in Joshua 21:45 *45 Not one word of all the good promises that the LORD had made to the house of Israel had failed; all came to pass.* The four-hundred-year-old promise along with those given through Moses were all fulfilled! Everything Moses assigned to Joshua was done. We, too, can be sure that none of God's good promises to us will fail (2 Corinthians 1:20). God is faithful and cannot lie. He is also able to do above and beyond all that He has promised in His Word (Ephesians 3:20).

1 At that time Joshua summoned the Reubenites and the Gadites and the half-tribe of Manasseh, 2 and said to them, "You have kept all that Moses the servant of the LORD commanded you and have obeyed my voice in all that I have commanded you. 3 You have not forsaken your brothers these many days, down to this day, but have been careful to keep the charge of the LORD your God. 4 And now the LORD your God has given rest to your brothers, as he promised them. Therefore turn and go to your tents in the land where your possession lies, which Moses the servant of the LORD gave you on the other side of the Jordan. Joshua 22:1-4

Biblical scholars estimate that Israel had been at war for about seven years taking the Promised Land. The warriors who had left their families beyond the Jordan had kept their promise and were now to return to their homes. I can't imagine how much they must have missed their wives and children.

They had gained the spoils of warfare for their service and sacrifice. They went home wealthy, but they were instructed to share that wealth with those who had stayed behind (verse 8). We see that principle with Moses in Numbers 31:27 and later with David in 1 Samuel 30:24. Those who stayed behind were busy caring for the flocks, building homes, and planting fields which the warriors would enjoy when they returned. The concept is very much like that of the body of Christ concept of the Apostle Paul in 1 Corinthians 12. We are all a part of one another. Each role is important. While some appear more glorious, without others in less glorious roles, they could not do what they do. Unlike the world, the people of God are interdependent. Instead of seeking one's own good, we are to seek the good of all (1 Corinthians 12:7). We are blessed to share the abundance God has given to us.

⁵ Only be very careful to observe the commandment and the law that Moses the servant of the LORD commanded you, to love the LORD your God, and to walk in all his ways and to keep his commandments and to cling to him and to serve him with all your heart and with all your soul." Joshua 22:5 Moses' one important command to them before they departed was that they be careful to observe the commandment and the law he had given them. Which commandment was that? It was the one Jesus said was the most important command: to love the LORD your

God (Matthew 22:37). If they do that, they will walk in all His ways, keep His commandments, cling to Him, and serve Him with all their heart and all their soul (Luke 10:25-28). That is the one command that we too must keep in the forefront of our hearts and minds.

Israelite devotion was never a matter of cold conformity to a code of rules, any more than Christian discipleship is. It is not external but deeply personal at root. Keeping Yahweh's rules is an expression of love for Yahweh's person.[xix] To "cling to Him" reminds me of that very intimate image from Song of Songs where they ask, *"Who is that coming up out of the wilderness leaning on her beloved"* (8:5a)?

They did not have the many blessings that we have today such as the revelation of Jesus, the printed Word in their hands, the indwelling presence of the Holy Spirit, of the volumes of worship music we have today. But they had seen the mighty hand of God. If they were ten-years-old when they left Egypt after seeing God show Himself more powerful than all Egypt's gods, then they would have seen the parting of the Red Sea, the provision of manna in the wilderness, the Law given to Moses on fiery Sinai, the water from a rock, the way God defeated their enemies, the death of their fathers for disobedience and murmuring, and now fulfillment of the promise to Abraham. They would then be fifty-seven years of age.

When they return to their allotted land, they will have the priests living in their midst who can remind them of the laws given to Moses. That generation stayed faithful as long as Joshua and the elders of that time lived (Judges 2:7). With all that God has given us and revealed to us in Jesus, will we cling to Him and love the LORD with all our heart and soul? Will we walk in all His ways? Will we finish the tasks that are assigned to us and take all the land God has for us?

All seemed to go so well to this point, but there was one more test. *[10] And when they came to the region of the Jordan that is in the land of Canaan, the people of Reuben and the people of Gad and the half-tribe of Manasseh built there an altar by the Jordan, an altar of imposing size. [11] And the people of Israel heard it said, "Behold, the people of Reuben and the people of Gad and the half-tribe of Manasseh have built the altar at the frontier of the land of Canaan, in the region about the Jordan, on the side that belongs to the people of Israel." [12] And when the people of Israel heard of it, the whole assembly of the people of Israel gathered at Shiloh to make war against them.* Joshua 22:10-12

This is a lesson on the all too frequent problem of misunderstanding from a lack of clear communication and making assumptions. Many of the problems within the church could be resolved if we did not jump to conclusions before sitting down and calmly discussing the situation at hand to understand one another's intentions and purposes.

[16] "Thus says the whole congregation of the LORD, 'What is this breach of faith that you have committed against the God of Israel in turning away this day from following the LORD by building yourselves an altar this day in rebellion against the LORD? Joshua 22:16 Any other altar other than that in the temple was forbidden by Moses (Deuteronomy 12:4,5; 13,14). The Israelites understood from their past that the sins of one person affect everyone else. This is one answer to why the innocent suffer. Adam and Eve's sin caused the entire human race to suffer for we as their offspring inherit their sinful nature (Romans 5:12). The Israelites had seen what happened at Peor, when idolaters caused a plague on the nation. That was only stopped by a spear through the disobedient couple (Numbers 25:6-9). They suffered defeat because of Achan's greed and disobedience (Joshua 7:11).

Church, we cannot say that just because only one lung has cancer that we are ok. Sin, like cancer, spreads and affects the whole congregation (2 Corinthians 5:6).

While their assumption was wrong, their reasoning was correct. That is often the case in church conflicts. Both sides were well meaning. That is why communication is so important, and that is what will solve this problem. Without it many souls would have needlessly perished, just as many church attendees would be wounded or leave when misunderstandings are not dealt with in a godly way. That is why Matthew 18 is so important. Jesus gave us a pattern of communication to understand one another and even deal with sin among us.

No one is an island. What each of us does affects all the rest of us. If each of us will be done with sin in our life and cling to the Lord and walk in the Spirit, the LORD can do great things with us as a congregation. The blessing of fruitfulness will flow, and I don't mean physical prosperity. I mean opportunities to touch others with the love of Jesus.

The eastern tribes responded, *22 "The Mighty One, God, the LORD! The Mighty One, God, the LORD! He knows; and let Israel itself know! If it was in rebellion or in breach of faith against the LORD, do not spare us today 23 for building an altar to turn away from following the LORD. Or if we did so to offer burnt offerings or grain offerings or peace offerings on it, may the LORD himself take vengeance.* Joshua 22:22,23 The defense of the eastern tribes begins with an affirmation, repeated for emphasis. *Elohim El YHWH!* They were declaring that the eternal God of Israel is the only God. They were saying their hearts were one with the rest of the nation in worshiping God alone. They even declare that if it was an altar to another god they would deserve to die. Then they began to explain the intention of the altar.

24 No, but we did it from fear that in time to come your children might say to our children, 'What have you to do with the LORD, the God of Israel? 25 For the LORD has made the Jordan a boundary between us and you, you people of Reuben and people of Gad. You have no portion in the LORD.' So your children might make our children cease to worship the LORD. Joshua 22:24-25 They explained their concern that in the future generations those who were on the western side of the Jordan might forbid those who were on the eastern side access to the tabernacle with its altar. They knew that would be disastrous for them. So, they set up a witness to remind the western tribes that they were one with them. In essence it was exactly the opposite of what the western tribes had assumed. It was not forsaking the God of Israel, but a witness of their dedication to Him for future generations.

29 Far be it from us that we should rebel against the LORD and turn away this day from following the LORD by building an altar for burnt offering, grain offering, or sacrifice, other than the altar of the LORD our God that stands before his tabernacle!" Joshua 22:29 Now that the real purpose of the altar was made clear, Israel thought it was a good thing. War was averted. Everyone was at peace. The nation was wholeheartedly following the LORD, walking in the fear of the LORD, and desiring out of love to worship Him alone. Sadly, it will only last for that generation. Their children will not have the same heart (Judges 2:10). Was it because the stories were not faithfully passed down? Was it that the nations who remained in the land presented tempting alternatives that appealed to the flesh? Or was it the prosperity they saw in their neighbors that attracted them to idolatry (Judges 2:2,3). Maybe it was all the above.

We must ask ourselves if we are faithfully passing our faith on to our children and their children. Is the idolatry of the world around us averting our attention and desires from the only One who can truly fill the void in our hearts? We see the decline of our nation and pray for revival, but it must begin in each of us. Is there an area of compromise in my life that is affecting the whole body? That is where revival begins. We need the fear of the LORD like they had, but also to combine it with faithfully communicating it to our children and their children (Deuteronomy 6:6,7).

31 And Phinehas the son of Eleazar the priest said to the people of Reuben and the people of Gad and the people of Manasseh, "Today we know that the LORD is in our midst, because you have not committed this breach of faith against the LORD. Now you have delivered the people of Israel from the hand of the LORD." Joshua 22:31 We can tell that the LORD is in our midst when we come together and resolve conflict discovering that what we are doing is from our zeal for the LORD. Just as the declaration that God is YHWH brought the tribes into unity, so the declaration that Jesus is Lord should bring the church into unity today (1 Corinthians 12:3). Those churches that do not agree with that declaration are really not churches but rather have become what the western tribes had assumed of the eastern tribes, worshiping other gods under the guise of Christianity. Other gods are not gods at all. They are pretenders trying to usurp Jesus rightful place as Lord over every area of our lives.

We should be as eager as they were to see our spiritual and physical families follow after God and take all the land that He has allotted to us. Let us be found faithful to communicate to our physical and spiritual children the mighty works of God in our lives, while living as an example of loving God with our whole hearts. We must do so for the glory of God, for the spiritual future of our children, and for the future of our nation.

Questions:

1 What can we learn from Manasseh's complaint?

2 How did cities of refuge open the gospel to a tribe?

3 How does it foreshadow Jesus?

4 How do we know we can count on God's promises?

5 Why should we share when God gives us abundance?

6 What command must we be faithful to obey?

7 What was the misunderstanding?

8 How was it resolved?

9 What does that teach us?

10 What did they fail to follow through with?

11 Relate that to our need for action today?

Cling to God Joshua 23

This is the next to the last message in Joshua. While this is an historical record of Israel's conquest of Canaan and distribution of their tribal lands, we have seen many spiritual analogies relating to our spiritual growth and claiming the spiritual land God has for us. We saw that it was an act of God that brought us into the kingdom in the parting of the Jordan. In the walls of Jericho falling, we saw God fights our battles if we will be obedient. We saw the consequences of compromise. We saw the importance of getting God's input in our decisions in the Gibeonite deception. And in the distribution of the land, we saw how God has appointed our lot in life and His faithfulness to His promises. Our last message in Joshua warned us to be faithful to pass on our faith to the following generations.

In our passage today, Joshua knows his time on earth is almost over and he wants to be sure the nation is faithful to do all that God has commanded. That should be our heart for our children and those whom we disciple. That is my heart for you.

* A long time afterward, when the LORD had given
rest to Israel from all their surrounding enemies, and
Joshua was old and well advanced in years, ² Joshua
summoned all Israel, its elders and heads, its judges and
officers, and said to them, "I am now old and well
advanced in years.* Joshua 23:1,2 Joshua knew he would
soon pass from this life, and so he called together the
leaders of Israel to share with them his concerns. In the
next chapter he will address the people and renew the
covenant before he dies. It is the leaders, the elders, judges,
and officers who will set the tone for the nation. While
people often elect someone like themselves, the rare person
of integrity can steer a people to become better. That is
what Moses had done, and Joshua followed in his mentor's
ways. Now that the people have dispersed into their own
sections of the country, it will be up to those leaders to
continue to lead the people in godly living. This was the
concern on Joshua's heart before he passed.

The text begins with the phrase, "a long time
afterward." Since Caleb took the land at eighty years of
age, if Joshua was about the same age and will pass at 110,
this may mean this took place thirty years after the
allotting the land to the tribes. Joshua had twenty to thirty
years to build, plant, harvest, and enjoy the fruit of his
labor and watch the growth of his posterity (Psalm 128:6).

*³ And you have seen all that the LORD your God
has done to all these nations for your sake, for it is the
LORD your God who has fought for you. ⁴ Behold, I have
allotted to you as an inheritance for your tribes those
nations that remain, along with all the nations that I have
already cut off, from the Jordan to the Great Sea in the
west. ⁵ The LORD your God will push them back before
you and drive them out of your sight. And you shall possess
their land, just as the LORD your God promised you.*
Joshua 23:3-5 Look what the Lord has done! There is a

song by that title. He healed my body; He healed my mind; He saved me just in time. O I'm gonna praise His name. Each day He's just the same. I'm gonna praise Him; Look what the Lord has done.

For the Israelites it was the amazing fulfillment of slavery to freedom and a homeland, victory over the enemies of God, homes and fields and wealth. What an amazing life they had lived. Is it not just as amazing for us? For us it is salvation of our souls, eternal life, separating us from the world, the fruits of the Spirit, the presence of Christ in us seeing us through the difficulties of life, the leading and comfort of the Holy Spirit, fruit that remains, and the expectation of our home in heaven (Psalm 103:2).

But like the Israelites, there is land allotted to us of which we have yet to take possession. While the Spirit gives me love and joy, I often miss out on these because I take my eyes off my Savior and focus on this fallen world (Hebrews 12:2). I can take the spiritual land if I will go to war, but I'm comfortable where I am. The LORD will go before me but being entertained and doing what I please are so much easier. Taking time to love others and get to know them and share Christ with them is demanding of my time, and it can be intimidating, even if I know Christ will go before me. To pray for them each day is time consuming. We face the same enjoyment of rest and compromise they faced (Galatians 6:9), which is why Joshua spoke the following verses.

6 Therefore, be very strong to keep and to do all that is written in the Book of the Law of Moses, turning aside from it neither to the right hand nor to the left, Joshua 23:6 Don't get soft! Be very strong to keep and to do what the Word commands us (2 Timothy 2:3). We are not under the laws of Moses, though the moral laws still apply to us. We have what the Law pointed to, the Messiah, Jesus (Luke

24:44)! And He gave us a new command. *"Love one another as I have loved you"* (John 15:12). *"Go into all the world and preach the gospel to every creature"* (Mark 16:15). *"Let the Word of God dwell in you richly"* (Colossians 3:16). *"Present your bodies as living sacrifices...Do not be conformed to the world but be transformed by the renewal of your mind"* (Romans 12:1,2). *"Endure hardness as a good soldier of Jesus Christ."* There are so many more commands in the New Testament. They are stated in a Greek tense called imperative. In other words, they are the things we must do in the power of the Spirit. When people say it is all by grace, I hope they are talking about salvation, because sanctification certainly requires us to be soldiers of the Lord Jesus and engage in a daily battle with the world, the flesh, and the devil (1 John 2:15-17).

Yes, the Lord goes before us and it is by grace that we continue to fight, but it is up to us to get up off our duffs and be obedient as Joshua was exhorting the Israelites to do. Notice he tells them to do ALL. The Bible is not a cafeteria where you take what you like and leave the rest, though that is how too many believers treat it (Joshua 1:8). God help us! And He will, if we get off our couches of comfort and engage in the battle. Sitting in your easy chair and saying, "It's all by grace," is an excuse to ignore the commands of Jesus our Savior! Christianity has been so soft pedaled and presented as a free ticket to heaven and nothing more. That is a damnable lie. It is enlisting in heaven's army. [24] *"Strive to enter through the narrow door. For many, I tell you, will seek to enter and will not be able.* Luke 13:24 We don't wage war like the world does. We fight on our knees (2 Corinthians 10:4,5). We take a lot of fire directed at us. We persevere and try harder because our Savior has gone before us as an example and His life in us empowers us (Romans 8:11).

Our retreats are temporary to be renewed so we can head back into battle against the world's strongholds, the ground the enemy holds in our minds, and against spiritual forces in the heavenly realms (Ephesians 6:12). Joshua told them to not turn aside from the Word to the right or the left (Deuteronomy 5:32). In other words, no compromise.

People ask me how to hear from God. We certainly can develop a spiritual ear for the Holy Spirit, and we should endeavor to do so, but we already have our instructions in the Word of God. If you aren't reading and studying and taking to heart the field manual, it is no wonder you don't know what God wants you to do. Get off the couch, get in your study chair, get some note paper or a diary and start learning what God expects you to do. Yes, He will help you, but don't say, "It's all be grace," while you spend your days doing as you please. A soldier who does as he pleases ends up dead or in the brig. Quit compromising and start training and listening for your orders. Did you notice we are losing the war in the USA? Our heroes are dying, and someone needs to take their place, or we'll all be in further retreat. Time for the church to wake up and take a stand.

7 that you may not mix with these nations remaining among you or make mention of the names of their gods or swear by them or serve them or bow down to them, Joshua 23:7 Here is our problem. Joshua was saying don't mix it up with the heathen so that you start talking about their gods (Psalm 16:4). You know what their gods are. Listen to what the popular people of the world promote. They identify them. The number one god for most people is self. A close second is possessions, followed by fame, and making a name for oneself.

I hesitate to put sports in this mix as many players honor God. But I can say that if you know more about the players' names than you do Bible characters, if you know more about their stats than you do Bible references, if you are more excited about game time than you are worshiping God, your priorities are out of whack. Do you think you will talk about any of those things in heaven? Eternity looms before us brothers and sisters.

8 but you shall cling to the LORD your God just as you have done to this day. Joshua 23:8 Here is the solution. Cling, cleave, hold tightly to the LORD you God. *"You shall cling to the Lord your God just as you have done to this day." This verb is used frequently by Moses in Deuteronomy and by Joshua in 22:8. It is perhaps the strongest adhesive verb in the Old Testament and is used in Genesis 2:24 to describe marriage. The man is to "hold fast to his wife," cling to her, stick fast to her, so that they become "one flesh." The word speaks, then, of total commitment, loyal devotion, and deep personal affection.* [xx] The world will always temp us to let go and grab something temporal that promises but never delivers.

Hebrews 2:1 is similar: *1 Therefore we must pay much closer attention to what we have heard, lest we drift away from it.* The language is of a boat securely tied to a dock. What they had heard were the laws God delivered to Moses and the testimony of God's holiness and faithfulness. Moses is warning them, and we have the same warning, that there is a temptation to relax our grip, to loosen the knot, to slowly without realizing it start drifting away from our commitment to God.

Those Israelites had been faithful to that point. They had forsaken everything to do God's will and take the land for seven long years of battles. They had seen amazing things as God fought for them, but most of the battles were sword to sword, slugging it out, bloody, hard fought and full of sweat. I don't blame them for wanting to rest instead of finishing the job. But Joshua is about to warn them what will happen if they don't. The warning is for us if we don't fight on and continue to *cling* to Jesus (John 12:26).

9 For the LORD has driven out before you great and strong nations. And as for you, no man has been able to stand before you to this day. 10 One man of you puts to flight a thousand, since it is the LORD your God who fights for you, just as he promised you. Joshua 23:9,10 Joshua is reminding them of what the LORD has done in driving out the nations that were more powerful than the Jews and yet the Jews were like supermen to them. They were so victorious it would have been a temptation to think they were mighty in their own strength (John 15:5).

We sometimes get to thinking that our salvation and progress toward sanctification is all just our effort, forgetting that it was grace that drew us and grace that keeps us. That doesn't mean that we don't make every effort to cooperate (2 Peter 1:5), but rather it recognizes that our efforts would be nothing without the abundance of grace we receive.

The enemy of our soul is much more powerful than we are. We are in similar sandals to these to whom Joshua is speaking. We are victorious in Christ, but don't let it go to your head. The enemy has not overwhelmed you only because Jesus has helped you to stand (Romans 8:31).

11 Be very careful, therefore, to love the LORD your God. 12 For if you turn back and cling to the remnant of these nations remaining among you and make marriages with them, so that you associate with them and they with you, 13 know for certain that the LORD your God will no longer drive out these nations before you, but they shall be a snare and a trap for you, a whip on your sides and thorns in your eyes, until you perish from off this good ground that the LORD your God has given you. Joshua 23:11-13 Because it is God who defeated our enemies who were stronger than us, we had better be very careful to love the LORD our God. This implies intentionality and effort (Deuteronomy 6:5). If we turn away from the LORD and start clinging to these nations and intermarry with the people still in the land and making associations with them (meaning ungodly people), the LORD will no longer fight for us. Just as the word "cling" is a picture of marital commitment to the LORD in verse 8, here it is a deep relationship and commitment to the idol worshiping nations. Those compromises for wealth or lust will only end up becoming a trap. They will be a whip on our side and thorns in our eyes. Then we will be the ones who perish.

The application was probably clear to you as you read it. Compromise with the world, marry the ungodly, go into business with the wicked, adopt the ways of this world and we fall under the curse (Psalm 7:11; 9:17). God wants us to love and cling to Him alone because He loves us and wants to bless us. But if we backslide and there is no difference between us and the world, why should we receive His blessings? Why not rather give us the judgments the world receives? I keep hearing that in the research polls the difference between the world and the church in many areas of life is negligible. We have failed to heed this warning.

14 "And now I am about to go the way of all the earth, and you know in your hearts and souls, all of you, that not one word has failed of all the good things that the LORD your God promised concerning you. All have come to pass for you; not one of them has failed. Joshua 23:14 Joshua knows he is about to die. All earth is experiencing the entropy that came with the curse (Romans 8:20,21). Our bodies are not exempt no matter how godly we are. He considered all the promises of God to Israel fulfilled. There was much yet to be done, but God had kept His side of the promises. The Jews could continue to stand on the Word of God and expect the promises to be fulfilled.

I believe we can say that God has not failed in any of the promises He has given us. There is much yet for us to do as well, and God has promised to help us, and we too can declare His faithfulness. But let us continue to trust in His great and wonderful promises.

Think back on all you have experienced of God's rich mercy and awesome covenantal grace thus far. Think of where you were when God found you, the circumstances of your new birth, the assurance of sins forgiven, your increasing deliverance from the world, the flesh, and the devil, your growth in grace and godliness, the progressive restoration of the image of God in you. They are all testimony to what the Lord our God has done for us in Christ. But they also motivate us to recognize that no faith can be strong if it is not growing, no virtue will be safe if it is not enthusiastic, and none of us will be secure if we are not daily dependent on God's mercy and grace, made ours in the Word and by the Spirit. Joshua's backward look is not an exercise in nostalgic self-indulgence. His theme song is not "I believe in yesterday." His call is to find fresh courage and focus from the past, to keep trusting and obeying the God of battles already won for his continuing victorious provision in all that lies ahead.[xxi]

15 But just as all the good things that the LORD your God promised concerning you have been fulfilled for you, so the LORD will bring upon you all the evil things, until he has destroyed you from off this good land that the LORD your God has given you, 16 if you transgress the covenant of the LORD your God, which he commanded you, and go and serve other gods and bow down to them. Then the anger of the LORD will be kindled against you, and you shall perish quickly from off the good land that he has given to you." Joshua 15,16 Joshua gave a final warning to the leaders. God was faithful, but now He expects us to be faithful (1 Corinthians 4:2). And just as He was faithful to bless us when we obey, so He will also be faithful to punish us if we rebel. He gave us the land we possess, and He can take it away. If we are so rebellious as to worship other gods, we will perish quickly from off the good land He has given us. Joshua was just restating the blessing and curses the LORD spoke through Moses in Deuteronomy 28. He gave the Amorites and Canaanites 400 years to repent because they knew so little of God (Genesis 15:16). But we who know who God is and of His love and faithfulness are expected to be faithful now. God will not have as much patience with those who know better.

The same battle is before us today. Will we be satisfied with the LORD, or will we chase after the lures the world tempts us with? Their deception is powerful, and we must stay ever vigilant, or we will lose out on the blessings while we run after delusions that in the end will consume us. We see it happen to others and think we are more dedicated, but the enemy is subtle (Genesis 3:1). He watches for our weak moments. That is why Joshua is using terms like "do all" and "cling" and "be very careful." The enemy is still in the land. We don't wrestle against flesh and blood but against spiritual powers. The Word of God is our sword and faith is our shield (Ephesians 6:16,17). It is by living the Word and standing on its promises that we overcome and remain strong. The battle is not over until we see Him face to face and hear Him say, *"Well done, good and faithful servant… enter into the joy of your Lord."* Matthew 25:21

Questions:
1 What was on Joshua's heart and why?
2 What had the Lord done for them? For us?

3 What detracts us from taking all our land?
4 What were they to keep and do? Us?
5 How can "it's all by grace" be an excuse?
6 What are the gods/idols of this world?
7 What does "cling to the Lord" imply?
8 How did we get this far in our spiritual journey?
9 What must we be careful to do?
10 What was Joshua's final warning? Application?

Choose! Joshua 24

We have come to the conclusion of the book of Joshua which includes Joshua's farewell challenge and his death. We have seen the faithfulness of God to keep His promises *and* His justice upon hardened hearts, both of the pagans and within the nation of Israel. They are about to receive a final warning that is applicable to us as well.

[1] Joshua gathered all the tribes of Israel to Shechem and summoned the elders, the heads, the judges, and the officers of Israel. And they presented themselves before God. [2] And Joshua said to all the people, "Thus says the LORD, the God of Israel, 'Long ago, your fathers lived beyond the Euphrates, Terah, the father of Abraham and of Nahor; and they served other gods. Joshua 24:1-2 Joshua again gathered the leaders of Israel before God at Shechem. This was the place where God had promised the land to Abraham four hundred years before (Genesis 12:6,7). The promise had come to pass. They came together not before Joshua but before God. That is what we do each time we gather.

I think we could call this his second farewell address. He began the speech with the prophetic introduction, *"Thus says the LORD, the God of Israel,"* which tell us this is prophecy. Was God speaking to Joshua, or was Joshua referring to Scripture? In either case he could say, "Thus says the LORD!" Because this is a recounting of things Moses received from the LORD. The preacher faithfully summarizing the clear message from God's Word can say, "Thus says the LORD," because God speaks through His Word.

The first words from the LORD were to remind them of their origin. Their patriarch Abraham was called out of paganism. Joshua began there because the theme of the message is to stay faithful to God and shun the idolatry of the nations around them. If you are here today there was probably a time when God called you out of idolatry.

3 Then I took your father Abraham from beyond the River and led him through all the land of Canaan, and made his offspring many. I gave him Isaac. Joshua 24:3 The physical children of Abraham were Ishmael, Isaac, and the children of Keturah. But Isaac was the son of promise. When God says He made Abraham's offspring many, we learn from the Apostle Paul that God is speaking of those with the faith of Abraham, faith to leave behind the idolatry of their clan and follow God wherever He leads. Abraham is the father of the people of faith (Romans 4:16,17; 9:8; Galatians 3:29).

God gave Abraham Isaac. It was not a natural birth. Sarah was well beyond the age childbearing. It was a supernatural birth that was a gift from God (Romans 4:19,20). Without that gift there would have never been Israel. God is emphasizing their miraculous origin and His plan for them. God is just as involved in each of our lives (Psalm 139:16).

4 And to Isaac I gave Jacob and Esau. And I gave Esau the hill country of Seir to possess, but Jacob and his children went down to Egypt. Joshua 24:4 Jacob and Esau went their separate ways. Esau was the father of the Edomite people. Israel had already encountered the Edomites. An Edomite would rule over them in the future,

Herod the Great. But Jacob's family, led by Joseph, lived in bondage in Egypt for 400 years. Though subjugated they multiplied and became a mighty nation (Acts 7:6).

5 And I sent Moses and Aaron, and I plagued Egypt with what I did in the midst of it, and afterward I brought you out. Joshua 24:5 Then God sent Moses and Aaron to deliver the people. They knew the story well because their fathers could tell of it firsthand, and probably often did. God showed His superiority over the gods of Egypt by turning them into plagues. The Nile was worshiped, so it became blood. Each plague dealt with something they worshiped. That was a not-so-subtle message that what they worshiped was not blessing them but instead was cursing them. The God of Israel showed He was superior to all the gods of Egypt, though Egypt had the secular power and exploited the Hebrews. Perhaps that was a message as well, for the Israelites would experience the same thing in the promised land. Nations would subjugate them for a time, but that does not mean their enemies' gods are greater than YHWH. It means the Israelites were unfaithful to God. God's mighty hand delivered them from Egypt and will deliver them again when they turn to Him (Zechariah 1:3).

The new covenant does not promise us that we will rule or even that we will be free from being oppressed. Most of the first century Christians were slaves. Many of the slaves in America were believers and sang spiritual songs as they labored. The hope of the new covenant is not in conditions of this life, but in eternal life we experience in Jesus. Abraham was seeking a city whose builder and maker is God (Hebrews 11:10). The old covenant promises of protection and prosperity were a physical picture of the spiritual promises that are ours in Jesus and which see us through the physical conditions of our short lives (Romans 8:35-37; 1 Corinthians 10:13).

6 "'Then I brought your fathers out of Egypt, and you came to the sea. And the Egyptians pursued your fathers with chariots and horsemen to the Red Sea. 7 And when they cried to the LORD, he put darkness between you and the Egyptians and made the sea come upon them and cover them; and your eyes saw what I did in Egypt. Joshua 24:6,7a The miraculous salvation of God in the nation's past would give them hope for conflicts in the future. What has God done in your past? How should that affect the way you see future conflict or trials? That is a good reason to keep a journal. We too easily forget how God brought us through what we thought was a hopeless situation.

7b And you lived in the wilderness a long time. Joshua 24:7b Did you notice the absence of the reason they were in the desert a long time? Did you notice that all their murmuring is not even mentioned? There is no mention of the compromise and idol worship at Baalpeor, or the revolt at Mount Sinai and the golden calf, or Korah's rebellion. That is grace! The older generation has died. The younger generation was faithful, so the sins of their fathers were not brought up. Surely, they were aware of what happened, being witnesses to most if not all their parents' failures (Ezekiel 18:20).

8 Then I brought you to the land of the Amorites, who lived on the other side of the Jordan. They fought with you, and I gave them into your hand, and you took possession of their land, and I destroyed them before you. 9 Then Balak the son of Zippor, king of Moab, arose and fought against Israel. And he sent and invited Balaam the son of Beor to curse you, 10 but I would not listen to Balaam. Indeed, he blessed you. So I delivered you out of his hand. Joshua 24:8-10 There were more victories because of the LORD being for them. Even with spiritual warfare taking place against them, God made them victorious. And so will it be with us in our spiritual battles,

186

for in Christ Jesus we are more than conquerors (Romans 8:37)!

¹¹ And you went over the Jordan and came to Jericho, and the leaders of Jericho fought against you, and also the Amorites, the Perizzites, the Canaanites, the Hittites, the Girgashites, the Hivites, and the Jebusites. And I gave them into your hand. ¹²And I sent the hornet before you, which drove them out before you, the two kings of the Amorites; it was not by your sword or by your bow. Joshua 24:11,12 The conquest of the nations within the land was the next example of God's faithfulness. It was because the LORD fought for them, not because they had forces superior to the Amorites. In the record of the conquest, we don't read of the hornets attacking cities. This tells us it was a metaphor or there was a lot more going on than the record reveals.

¹³ I gave you a land on which you had not labored and cities that you had not built, and you dwell in them. You eat the fruit of vineyards and olive orchards that you did not plant.' Joshua 24:13 On top of all the faithfulness and grace just mentioned, they received homes and fields, vineyards, and olive groves. God kept His promise to Abraham in ways greater than Abraham would have imagined. *Their entire history is the record of God's overflowing covenant grace, as is ours.*[xxii]

The same will be true for us when we cross the Jordan of death and enter our heavenly dwellings that the Lord has been preparing for us (John 14:1,2). Even now we walk in victory not because we are so disciplined, but because of the gift of the Holy Spirit and the power of our Savior's life who has made us new creations through the death, burial, and resurrection of Jesus. The promised land of faith is ours in Him (Ephesians 1:3). And we know that He who began a good work in us will be faithful to complete it on the day of Jesus Christ (Philippians 1:6).

Would you consider writing your own account of how good God has been to you? Write it as if the LORD was recounting your story to you. You can leave out all your failures just like God did for them. Mine started like this: I put you in a home where you would hear my Word constantly. I spoke to your heart when you were just five-years-old and called you to be mine. Countless times I saved you from the consequences of bad choices and directed your life in mercy and grace. I walked with you through the painful times and comforted your heart. I listened to your prayers and answered. I met with your Bible study group and let you all know my holy, loving, presence in a way that would change your life. That would be the highlights until about 16 years of age. I did finish writing the rest. Would you write yours out as an act of worship, reminding yourself how grateful you should be to God for His abundant grace?

14 "Now therefore fear the LORD and serve him in sincerity and in faithfulness. Put away the gods that your fathers served beyond the River and in Egypt, and serve the LORD. Joshua 24:14 Because of all the goodness, guidance, blessings, and grace we have received, we should now therefore fear the LORD. That is to be in reverential awe of Him. Realizing how prone we are to err; we should fear getting out of His will and the discipline we would incur if we should be ungrateful (Philippians 2:8).

And serve Him with sincerity and faithfulness. That means with a whole heart in a consistent manner. They must have still kept the mini-idols that came out of Egypt with their fathers. After all their experiences of God's divine intervention on their behalf, what in the world were they doing with those gods? But before we become too harsh with them, we should search our own hearts. Are there gods we inherited that we keep around, gods we depend on such as alcohol, entertainment, compromising behavior or thought life, trust in wealth or our job, home, car, beauty, just about anything can be put before God. Instead of thanking Him for the good things and using them in moderation, we can depend on them for our happiness and comfort. We can say we trust God when we really trust other things (Proverbs 3:5). The test comes when we are prompted by the Holy Spirit to let go of them. Then we see how much we look to them for our pleasure. Food is a big one. You realize that when you attempt to fast and pray. If you think something may have taken the supremacy over God in your life, try setting it aside for a week such as some people do in the season of Lent. Then you will see your real relationship with it. If you are dependent on it, put it away until you can put it in its proper place. If the Jesus is not Lord of all my life, then he is not really my Lord at all[xxiii],(Matthew 6:24).

15 And if it is evil in your eyes to serve the LORD, choose this day whom you will serve, whether the gods your fathers served in the region beyond the River, or the gods of the Amorites in whose land you dwell. But as for me and my house, we will serve the LORD." Joshua 24:15 Decision time! Choose between those false gods or the God who did all that is mentioned in verses 2 through 13. The false gods only provide momentary satisfaction and end up costing more than you imagined. Time to choose. They were settling in as a nation, and if there were people who served another god, it was time for them to leave. Joshua gave no doubt where he and his family stood. What an inspirational challenge! I hope we can all say the same.

In verses 16-18 the people of Israel promised to serve the God who had done all those great things for them. *19 But Joshua said to the people, "You are not able to serve the LORD, for he is a holy God. He is a jealous God; he will not forgive your transgressions or your sins. 20 If you forsake the LORD and serve foreign gods, then he will turn and do you harm and consume you, after having done you good."* Joshua 24:19,20 Here is Joshua's answer to them and to us. You can't do it. You aren't able. God is holy and jealous, and He won't just look the other way when you sin. His holiness demands justice. Yes, He is love, but He is also righteous and just. If you forsake Him and go after some false god after all He has done for you, after vowing not to, what do you think justice should be? A little slap on the hand? No! Just as He has blessed you, in the same proportion He will deal to you the harm you deserve (Romans 6:23). He will consume you! Don't think for a minute you can receive all His blessings and go whoring after some other god and get away with it. Friendship with the world is enmity with God (James 4:4). PERIOD! And you won't handle being God's enemy very well!

²¹ And the people said to Joshua, "No, but we will serve the LORD." Joshua 24:21 Joshua just told them they can't do it. Now they respond, "Yes, we can!" "When you think you can do it you already blew it!" Sounds like Peter telling Jesus that if no one else follows, he will (Matthew 26:35). I hear a rooster crowing.

They will be faithful while Joshua lived. But after he dies, they will do exactly what they promised never to do. What God is trying to teach us is that we can't do it in our own strength (John 15:5). We need the help of God moment by moment. We need our minds renewed by His Word (Romans 12:2). We need the fellowship that reminds us to stay on track and challenges us when we fail. We need the conviction of the Holy Spirit to turn us toward Jesus in every situation we face (John 16:8).

In verses 22 to 28 the people vow to follow serve the Lord and obey His voice. Then Joshua told them to get rid of the little gods their fathers took out of Egypt. Joshua is telling them what Moses told them and repeating what he told them in verse 14. He asked, "Do you mean what you are saying? Then once and for all time throw away your little idols and *incline your hearts to the LORD.*"

This message is just as real today as it ever was. We go to church, give our tithes, call ourselves good Christians, but the secret little idols that we spend the weekdays on have never been put away. What keeps us from keeping Jesus first in private times? What are you convicted about? If it is a real issue, I don't have to point it out, the Holy Spirit already has. Get rid of it once and for all!

They renewed the covenant again and Moses set up a large stone as a reminder of the commitment they voiced. I believe this is the fourth time they did so in Joshua.

29 After these things Joshua the son of Nun, the servant of the LORD, died, being 110 years old. 30 And they buried him in his own inheritance at Timnath-serah, which is in the hill country of Ephraim, north of the mountain of Gaash. Joshua 24:29,30 I witnessed many saints who have gone on to glory: Ed Reyes, Connie Logan, the Crawfords (Mr. and Mrs. Wayside), Ida Pierce, Bea Waters to name just a few of those who played such a major role in the outreach from Wayside Chapel. There are at least twenty more I could name. I have preached at their memorial services about how their lives honored God. We are but a vapor that appears for a time and then vanishes away (James 4:14), but what remains are the lives that have been drawn to Jesus through His life in us. We each should consider that before we leave this earth. How has the life of Jesus in us affected those we know and love?

A hero of the faith, Joshua, went to his heavenly reward. His testimony was that he did all that Moses had commanded him (Joshua 11:15). It reminds me of the death of Bill Bright and Billy Graham. They are no longer present, but they and those whom I mentioned previously are more alive now than they ever were while they were here. Their old bodies will be replaced with heavenly ones (Philippians 3:21). In that great cloud of witnesses, they are cheering us on (Hebrews 12:1). We have their examples and writings to encourage us as we run our race. It is now our turn to look into the face of God and shine with God's glory (1 Corinthians 3:18).

31 Israel served the LORD all the days of Joshua, and all the days of the elders who outlived Joshua and had known all the work that the LORD did for Israel. Joshua 24:31 Every generation needs a personal encounter with God. We cannot live on our parent's faith. God has no grandchildren.

32 As for the bones of Joseph, which the people of Israel brought up from Egypt, they buried them at Shechem, in the piece of land that Jacob bought from the sons of Hamor the father of Shechem for a hundred pieces of money. It became an inheritance of the descendants of Joseph. Joshua 24:32 Before Joseph died in Egypt, he had the people promise to take his bones with them back to Israel (Hebrews 11:22). He reminded them of the promise God made to Abraham, Isaac, and Jacob. A small pyramid in Goshen that had been carefully opened was discovered by archeologists. Unlike the raiding of the other pyramids, this was a work done in the open and with great care. The fragments of a statue within appear to be of a Hebrew with a coat of many colors. [xxiv]

33 And Eleazar the son of Aaron died, and they buried him at Gibeah, the town of Phinehas his son, which had been given him in the hill country of Ephraim. Joshua 24:33 Eleazar, son of Aaron, also died and was buried. His son would be high priest and carry on the prescribed duties. After all the elders passed, the nation entered the era we call Judges. Sadly, the following generation did not stay faithful. For 400 years the nation had ups and downs depending on their faithfulness to God or lack thereof. When they turned to idolatry, God disciplined them through foreign invaders. He would raise up godly judges to bring them back and restore them time after time. Joshua's warning came to pass. The defining statement of those four hundred years was that every man did what was right in his own eyes (Judges 17:6). In other words, they set aside the laws of God and made up their own rules. Is it any different today? And though we have the Spirit of God indwelling us today, their story seems to be our story as well.

Joshua was successful because he believed God's promise given in the first chapter. *8 This Book of the Law shall not depart from your mouth, but you shall meditate on it day and night, so that you may be careful to do according to all that is written in it. For then you will make your way prosperous, and then you will have good success.* Joshua 1:8 The promise is for all who are willing to believe the Word and act on it. It is for those who declare, *"As for me and my house, we will serve the Lord."* What about you? Will you declare it with me? "As for me and my house, we will serve the LORD!" As Joshua declared, "You are unable to do it!" *But with God, all things are possible* (Matthew 19:26)!

Questions:
1 Why did God begin with the call to Abraham?
2 What had God done for them?
3 Why didn't he mention their failures?
4 What did Joshua say their response should be?
5 How did Joshua say we should serve God?
6 What choice did they have to make?
7 What did they promise? Have you made the same promise?
8 What was Joshua's response?

9 What was Joshua's testimony?

10 What happened after his death? Are we on the same trajectory?

---

[i] David Jackman-Preaching the Word - Joshua: People of God's Purpose.

[ii] ibid

[iii] ibid

[iv] Chambers, O. (1986). *My utmost for his highest: Selections for the year*. Grand Rapids, MI: Oswald Chambers Publications; Marshall Pickering; Oct. 30.

[v] Jesus justified breaking the Sabbath law of not working when His disciples at grain the pulled and hulled. He reasoned that David at the shewbread when His men were desperately hungry, and concluded that God desires mercy more than sacrifice. See Matthew 12:1-8

[vi] Jackman, David, *Preaching the Word - Joshua: People of God's Purpose.*

[vii] Hess, R. S. (1996). *Joshua: An Introduction and Commentary* (Vol. 6, p. 133). Downers Grove, IL: InterVarsity Press.

[viii] Joshua 6:2 – LORD all capitals is the English translation of YHWH. The man's words are YHWH speaking to Joshua.

[ix] See Judges 13:6, 22

[x] David Jackman, Preaching the Word - Joshua: People of God's Purpose

[xi] ibid

[xii] ibid

[xiii] Isaiah 45:11 (KJV) [11] Thus saith the LORD, the Holy One of Israel, and his Maker, Ask me of things to come concerning my sons, and concerning the work of my hands command ye me.

[xiv] *Jackman, Preaching the Word - Joshua: People of God's Purpose.*

[xv] John McNeill

[xvi] Jackman Preaching the Word - Joshua: People of God's Purpose.

[xvii] Chambers, O. (1986).*My Utmost for His Highest*. Grand Rapids, MI: Oswald Chambers Publications; Marshall Pickering.

[xviii] *Christian Age- The number of the cities of refuge*

[xix] Jackman, D. (2014).Joshua, People of God's Purpose. (R. K. Hughes, Ed.) (p. 185). Wheaton, IL: Crossway

[xx] ibid

[xxi] ibid

[xxii] ibid

[xxiii] Attributed to Augustine.

[xxiv] https://www.levitt.com/essays/joseph#identification

Other books by Pastor Paul Wallace:

Through the Bible Daily Devotional
Through the Bible Again volumes 1 and 2
Jesus Concealed in the Old Testament
John's Rabbi
Divine Messiah?
Preaching Through Genesis
Preaching Through Exodus
Preaching Through Isaiah
Preaching Through Zechariah
Preaching Through Matthew volumes 1 and 2
Preaching Through Luke
Preaching Through Acts
Preaching Through Romans
Preaching Through Ephesians
Preaching Through Colossians
Preaching Through Philippians
Preaching Through Hebrews
Preaching Through 1John
Preaching Through 2Peter, Jude, Revelation 1-5